"I suppose I'm nothing now. I don't belong anywhere."

Joanna looked at me with quiet authority. "Oh, but you are something. You are a Christian."

A Christian! How could I be a Christian? I was a Jew, and Jews did not become Christians! The very word was a contradiction of all that being Jewish meant.

In my confusion I let my mind wander back to relive that extraordinary moment when both the Old and New Testament had come together for me and I had gazed on a tapestry woven with great harmony and precision instead of a tangled mass of skeins. . . . God's forgiveness was the missing piece in the puzzle I had been searching for all along.

"Yes," I said slowly to Joanna. "You're right. I am a Christian." Then, as I realized fully what I was saying, "Oh, horrors!" I gasped. "What will my parents say?"

Other BALLANTINE/EPIPHANY titles

CHILD
OF THE
COVENANT
Michele Guinness

BALLANTINE BOOKS • NEW YORK

ISBN 0-345-32715-2

This edition published by arrangement with Hodder and Stoughton

Manufactured in the United States of America

First Ballantine Books/Epiphany Edition: October 1985

*For JOEL and ABIGAIL
children of the covenant who never tire*

Acknowledgements

By their support and encouragement more people have been involved in the writing of this story than I could begin to mention. But a special thanks to David Lewis and Sue Rosseter, who reading the original draft made me go home and start all over again—with many useful tips; to Marlene Stephenson, Julie Taylor, and Sue Elkins, my three typists who have worked like Trojans; to David Hughes, Vicar of Normanton Parish Church, who endured the constant disappearance of the church typewriter with much grace. I promised him an acknowledgement. Here it is!

I owe a great deal to my parents. Without their extraordinary courage and humour the tale could never have been told. My Canadian mother-in-law ruthlessly corrected my English grammar with the precision of a true colonial. I am indebted to her perfectionism and red pen!

My husband said he wished for no acknowledgement and that just about says everything about him. Only by the self-sacrificial nature of his love have I been able to write.

Glossary

Rosh Hashanah   The Jewish New Year
Yom Kippur   The Day of Atonement
Succoth   Booths, the Harvest Festival
Pesach   The Passover
Purim   The Feast of Esther
Chanukah   The Feast of the Dedication of the Temple
Shabbat   The Sabbath
Afikomen   The middle piece of the three matzos used in the Passover service (Symbolises the Paschal lamb)
Beth Din   Central body which dictates and regulates the dietary laws
Charoseth   Substance made of apples, wine and walnuts used at Passover and meant to resemble mortar
Chasidim   An ultra orthodox Jewish sect
Cheder - Hebrew classes
Chollah   Plaited Sabbath loaf
Chuckele   (Yiddish) "Pet"—term of endearment
Chuppah   Canopy of flowers under which Jews are married: a tradition dating back to their desert wanderings
Cohanim   The priests
Frumm   (Yiddish) very orthodox or religious
Gefüllte fish   Chopped (usually fried) fish balls, traditionally served on the Sabbath
Goyim   The Gentiles, or non-Jews
Haggadah   Service book used at the Passover (lit. "The narration")
Kaddish   Prayers recited at a funeral and house of mourning
Kiddush   The Sabbath prayer and service

Kosher According to the dietary laws

Matzo Unleavened bread

Menorah The nine-branched candelabra used at the feast of Chanukah

Minyan The ten men needed before any official prayers may be said.

Seder Instruction classes in Hebrew

Sheitel The wig worn by an orthodox Jewish woman

Shema The morning and evening prayers

Shivah The seven days of official mourning after a bereavement

Shofar The ram's horn

Siddur Jewish prayer book

Simcha A time of celebration

1

I do like pedigrees! They convey such a sense of con-tinuity and destiny, almost of immortality. My husband's is most impressive. He can boast of brewers, bankers, millionaires and even peers of the realm in his family tree. Would that mine were as illustrious! I could of course say that Abraham, the patriarch, was my goodness-knows-how-many-great-grandfather, that Moses must figure some-where, but that was a long, long time ago. Our recent history was not quite so brilliant, although it does have its moments.

"But you're not really British, are you?" people say to me, and it makes me mad. I want to wave my passport under their noses.

"As British as you are—well, almost."

I am the second generation to be born in this country and though I may not look the classic English rose, I feel very British as well as Jewish inside. This was the dream which inspired my great-grandparents. I am its fulfillment, or at least, I would have been, had not things turned out very differently from what we all expected.

I was twelve years old when my maternal great-grandparents died. I knew it was an event of major impor-tance for the family, because everyone wept, argued and fought in a way I had never seen before, but it did not particularly bother me as I hardly knew them. Fortnightly visits to their dark, melancholy house with its extraordinary smell of damp and lavender, had seemed more like a punishment than a pleasure. Great-grandpa never moved from his fireside chair. His black skullcap perched on his wizened little polished apple of a head, he would mutter to himself in Hebrew, plunging the piece of lemon up and down in his tea in a kind of rhythmical accompaniment. Great-grandma would be bent over the stove stirring some concoction in a huge copper pot, cackling merrily over some private source of amusement.

"Dirty jokes," my mother told me when she thought I was old enough to understand. "Your great-grandmother's sense of humor has always thrived on the basics of life." I did not have a clue what she meant.

"Come on my little chuckele," great-grandma would say. She always used that Yiddish term of endearment or its Geordie equivalent, "little pet", then nipped my cheek between her bony fingers until tears welled up in my eyes with the pain of it. "Eat up."

"But Grandma, I'm not hungry. I've already eaten."

"You want to grow into a big girl, don't you?"

"Not too big," interjected my mother. Mother's enormous size as a teenager was a family proverb, a warning to all of the dangers of great-grandma's cooking.

"Eat half," mother whispered to me, "and put the rest over there." She pointed to a pile of dirty plates at the end of the table. One more would not be noticed.

How I wish I had known then what I know now, what a wealth of adventure and experience lay behind that withered, shrivelled appearance. So many things I would have asked them, so many stories I would have begged to hear. But in all our many visits I never exchanged more than a sentence with them. The room was always so full of aunts, uncles and cousins chattering loudly all at once that I could hardly ever hear what they were saying. And when I did, it

2

was such a strange mixture of Yiddish and broken English with a Newcastle accent that I found it hard to understand anyway.

It was not until I was a teenager and spent occasional weekends with my grandmother, the sixth of their eight children, that I began to realise all my great-grandparents had been through.

One night, long after everyone else was asleep, I saw gran, in dressing-gown and curlers, slip into the kitchen for a last cigarette. I followed her and while she sat warming her hands round a hot cup of tea made her tell me about her parents.

"They came from Lithuania," she said, flicking ash into her saucer and watching it slowly disintegrate into the tea slops.

"Where?"

"Russia."

"Why did they come here?"

"They thought the streets were paved with gold, that a young man could grow rich and famous."

"And they couldn't in Russia?"

"Oh no. Tzar Nicholas, of 'Nicholas and Alexandra', you know . . ."

"They were baddies?"

"Not exactly, just weak. He allowed his Cossack soldiers to ride rough-shod over Jewish settlements, looting, pillaging, killing as they went. You were lucky to stay alive, let alone make a living or build a future for your children." Gran looked up, but not at me. In her eyes was the fond admiration of a little girl for her proud, handsome father.

He arrived without a penny in his pocket. The overcrowded boat offloaded its herd of immigrants on the Tyne Quay. "Name?" shouted an official. My great-grandfather looked round at his compatriots, each more lonely and bewildered than the last. It was he who was being spoken

3

to. He stated his name. The official looked blank. How many times would he have to repeat it, spell it, and what was it worth now anyway? He looked around for inspiration. A man was selling fish from a barrow on the quayside. Great-grandpa pointed to a pile of debris left behind by the filleting.

"Fish skin?" said the official quizzically.

"Fishkin," nodded great-grandpa, and set off with a new name into a new life.

"How did he meet great-grandma?"

The question startled gran out of her silence. A smile formed on her lips, which grew into a chuckle. "He was given an introduction to another Jewish family already living here. It was the accepted thing. After all, he was totally alone. He knew no one. Someone back at home had scribbled the address of a Landsleit, a distant relative long since settled in Newcastle, on a scrappy piece of paper. A name and address in your pocket was more valuable than gold. Mind you, father was not to know whether they were in any position to offer him assistance, but he was in luck. The gentleman in question was the local *shochet*, the ritual slaughterer, a man of learning and standing in the small community. He could teach him English, and provide him with a dowry which would start a business, for it just so happened there were many marriageable daughters in the family. But father never intended to marry mother. It was Kitty, her younger sister, he wanted. You should have seen her. She had violet eyes and long auburn hair."

"Then what happened? Why couldn't he have her?"

"She had an elder unmarried sister, and in those days you did what custom dictated."

"Is that why he and great-grandma argued so much?" I had learnt at an early age that not all the Yiddish I had heard them speak could be repeated in polite company.

Gran laughed. "Don't believe all you see," she said. "They enjoy their quarrels, it keeps their minds active.

4

And besides, they've always shared a bed, and that's saying something." Gran stubbed out her cigarette and was about to stand up.

"And did he forget Kitty?"

She sat down again, and went silent. "No, he never did," she said after a while. "Kitty married a worthless charlatan. They thought he was a count. What a match! But he was a nobody. He abandoned her during all her five pregnancies. She bore him four sons, then died giving birth to a daughter. I vividly remember the day the letter came telling us of her death. Father took it with him into his study and laid it on his desk. I crept in a few moments later. He had his head in his hands and was weeping bitterly."

The country of his adoption did not fail great-grandfather Fishkin. Like many of his kinsmen, he made his fortune in the rag trade. On a Saturday evening when the sun had set and the Sabbath was over, the doors of his vast old house were flung open and young Jews came from miles around to eat and dance. Festivities always ended at midnight on the dot when the pianist was issued with a final command, "Play 'God Save the King'." One night, my grandmother, too young to be allowed to attend at the time, was spying through the keyhole. A game of forfeits was under way, and that particular forfeit required the unlucky girl who had picked it to kiss the handsomest young man in the room. A striking young man stepped forward. "That's me, I believe. I'm the handsomest man in the room."

Gran drew in her breath and pressed her eye as closely to the hole as she could. "He is too," she thought. "I'll have him one day, and bring him down a peg or two." She did just that!

"Mother's own marriage made her a stickler about one thing," gran confided in me at another of our late night encounters in the kitchen. The stillness of the hour and a strong cup of tea always had a strangely liberating effect

5

on our conversation. "Any marriage could be made to work, whatever the circumstances." She paused, the steaming kettle in her hand poised over the teapot, and turned to look at me, as if debating whether to continue her story or not. Then her face relaxed into a grin and she giggled. "You'll never guess what I did on my wedding night. I ran away!"

"You what? Why?"

"Well I wasn't having any of . . . that, was I?"

"You mean, for all her apparent broad-mindedness great-grandma never actually told you about the facts of life?"

"She wouldn't have dreamed of it, but she did that night, when she found me on the doorstep."

"What did she say?"

"She sent me home to grandpa. Told me to get on with it, that I was lucky it wasn't an arranged marriage like hers or some of my friends'."

"What did you do?"

"Did as I was told, just as we all did and always have done, until she died. As brothers and sisters we've had our differences, but she kept the family together. Now I seem to be falling out with everyone. If only one of us had been more like her."

I waited in silence, not daring to interrupt her flow, desperately hoping that gran would explain what she meant. What was so special about that strange old lady? Gran sighed, swirled the teabags round in the pot with her spoon in a distracted sort of way, poured the steaming black liquid into a cup and then sipped thoughtfully.

"You see, she was a good Jew. I mean she was a really good woman." I must have looked quizzical.

"Well, for example, after she died and we were sitting *Shivah* for her, you know, the ritual one week of mourning, one evening just before prayers your mother happened to tell us that whenever she went to the house mother sent

6

her down the road with a hot meal for a certain Miss Weinberg, an old lady who was infirm and bedridden.''

"You took hot meals to Miss Weinberg? So did I!"

"So did I, but she made me promise not to tell anyone!"

"Me too!"

Well, it turned out that each of the grandchildren had taken meals to Miss Weinberg every time they called and that in all probability Miss Weinberg had had a good hot meal every day of her life. That was mother all right, that was her Judaism, she lived and breathed it. Gran stared wistfully into her empty teacup.

"I'm not like that," she said slowly. "I try, God knows I try. I keep the festivals, I keep the laws, well most of them, I keep a strictly kosher kitchen, just as she taught me to. Have you ever had meat with dairy produce in this house? Of course not. But somehow it's not the same. She and Father, they were on familiar terms with the Almighty. They spoke to him like you speak to a friend. But I've never seen him like that. I can't. Life's far too complicated. My brother, your uncle Joe, he's a clever man, he reads, he studies the Torah, the Talmud and other holy Jewish writings, perhaps he can make sense of it all. Well," Gran started suddenly, "none of us has inherited their simple kind of faith and there's an end to it." She rinsed her cup and saucer without a word and then headed for the door. She stopped and turned round slowly. "Perhaps," she said thoughtfully, "perhaps it's something you're given when you specially need it, you know, in all the troubles they had to face. And perhaps with all this," she waved vaguely at her beautifully fitted kitchen, "we no longer need it, well not in the same way. Who knows?" She shook her head and disappeared into her bedroom. The door clicked shut and the still house seemed very cold and empty.

* * *

7

How can I describe my father's family? If I said that they were rich, romantic and prosperous, alas, it would merely be wishful thinking. They were from Latvia, now Poland, and of much less volatile, more serious and solid stock. In fact, relationships with fellow Lithuanian and Austrian immigrants were often severely strained. They might well all be Jews but there were still marked differences.

"Ach, a Pole she wants to marry, a Litvak," my great-grandfather lamented when my mother told him of her choice.

Not all Jews have the Midas touch. My father's family proves it. That is not to say they did not dream of material glory, but somehow their dreams always disintegrated in the light of circumstances.

Great-uncle Isaac took a job on the railways and was not looking one day when a train passed by. Great-uncle Mark went gold prospecting in South Africa, found nothing and lost every penny he had in the first place. Their sister, my grandmother, followed them over here ostensibly to clean and keep house. She had already met and fallen in love with her future husband, but their parents thought it an unsuitable match. He was a mercenary and a mercenary's future is always unpredictable. She had been left a semi-cripple by a childhood fall and might not be the sort of wife a man needs. He pursued her to Britain, they were married, and my grandfather began to build the first chara-banc business in Teesside. He did very well too, until one night his partner disappeared with all the profits. If fate never smiled on my father's family, it actually seemed to leer at my grandfather, who was a gracious, gentle man.

Their eldest child, my aunt Vera, was the most glori-ously eccentric person I have ever met. She always wore purple, which was her favourite colour, and I mean wore purple—shoes, stockings, hat, gloves, even eyeshadow. When she bought shoes, another great passion of hers, she bought them in triplicate, one pair in purple, one pair in

8

gold and one pair in silver, if possible. I once asked her if I could borrow a pair of gloves for a special occasion. I imagined a neat little pile of three or four pairs, squeezed into the corner of a chest of drawers, as mine were. Instead, she opened her wardrobe door and began to heave at an enormous sack, which would not budge until we both pulled. She opened it, and taking a deep breath, heaved it upside down and tipped its contents on the floor. There before my eyes appeared the most enormous rainbow-coloured mound of gloves.

"Help yourself, darling," she panted, then chortled when she saw my face, "that is, if you can find a matching pair."

Money meant nothing to her (she is still the only person I have ever known to stew best grilling steak). But despite the love and generosity she showered on me I knew she was unhappy, and not just because she could not have children.

Uncle Solly was a surly man, unable to show affection, the only one to be amused by his own jokes.

"Why did she marry him?" I asked my father, after one of our regular Sunday afternoon visits. Their sniping and bickering had been worse than usual and aunt Vera seemed to have doubled the number of cream cakes she normally landed on my plate. I felt decidedly queasy. "Did she love him once?"

"Oh yes, at least she thought so. She was totally infatuated."

"And did he love her?"

"I don't know, dear, but I don't think so. He needed money badly, to help him finish his studies in medicine and set up in practice somewhere. In those days the only way to do that was to find a girl with a decent dowry." Father went quiet. He put down the medical journal he had been reading, and there was an expression of great sadness on his face. "Do you know," he said after a while, "that

9

so-and-so came to the house a few days before the wedding and said he wouldn't marry her unless father gave him two hundred pounds more."

"Did aunty Vera know all that?"

"Know it! She was standing outside the door with her ear to the keyhole."

"Then why did she do it? How could she?"

"Because," my mother intervened harshly, as if she had been through the conversation so many times that it wearied her, "your grandmother wanted a doctor for her daughter, and a doctor she'd have at any cost." Father nodded reluctantly. "But my word," continued my mother, with an air of private satisfaction, "did they live to regret it!"

Father waited for her to leave the room, then turned to me and said, "The day father's business collapsed, who do you suppose was the first on the doorstep demanding what he was promised?" I said nothing. I was horrified that anyone could be so callous. "But Solly got his money all right," Father continued, "every penny. Father begged and borrowed, then returned to the only skill he had ever learned back in Latvia, tailoring. He worked all day and sometimes all night too to pay off the debts he'd incurred. And he did it, because he was a man of his word, but it cost him his health. He was paralysed down one side for two years before he died. He was only fifty-five."

I looked at my father's face for some time, trying to imagine what depths of hatred for Uncle Solly must lie behind his distant expression, but he simply said, "You would have liked father so much. I wish he could have seen you three children."

I realised then how many of his own values were modelled on his father's. He seemed to me a man incapable of harbouring bitterness and rancour and I loved him for it. The shattering realisation of the wealth of regret and self-reproach which lay behind that controlled exterior dawned slowly and much much later.

My grandmother was desolate after my grandfather's death. She had no choice but to swallow her pride and move in with her daughter and son-in-law. She was never welcome in their sitting-room. She sat alone in her self-imposed imprisonment in one room of my aunt's large house, a frail little old lady with hunched shoulders and a permanently wrinkled forehead.

"They think I don't know that they fry bacon. Well I may not be what I once was but I still have a nose."

"Smoked beef, mother," my father would reassure her.

Nothing made her smile any more, not even my clowning, dressed up in her best Sabbath hats, with their long, drooping, birds-of-paradise feathers. The world had turned sour on her. One day she took the only revenge she could, and ended her own life.

Come to think of it, my family has quite a flair for posthumous revenge. Aunt Vera's will left every penny to her brother, my father; a fact which her husband, Uncle Solly found very hard to explain, and the solicitors found impossible to enforce.

So to my parents! Strange how one can never imagine one's own parents' romance. It seems a bit indecent that they should have their moment of passion, though we grant it to everyone else. My father said it happened like this.

He was at a Jewish wedding, which happens to be a very good hunting ground, as every Jew knows. He was fast approaching thirty, the age at which a man has had his fling and needs a bit of tender loving care, someone to warm his underwear in the morning, just like his mother did. He had rarely dated Jewish girls, but marriage was a different proposition, it had to be kosher! He was just dancing a suave little military two-step, when a lady's heel from behind lodged itself in his trouser turn-up and dragged both him and the lady in question to the floor. She was furious, he was charmed. With such an introduction what could the chivalrous gentleman do but prolong the acquaintance?

Mother was seventeen and terribly green. She had never been away from home, never set eyes on a boy who was not Jewish. Along came my father, all five-foot-three of him, and bowled her over with his charm and worldliness. And he was a doctor! Security and social status were no small carrot. Only one little cloud darkened the glorious horizon: he appeared to have little interest in Judaism, except in so far as the traditions reminded him of a happy childhood.

"But darling, there's been a war. I've seen suffering you would never have dreamed of. How can there be a God?"

"Don't talk like that. You can't really mean it."

"Oh, but I do! 'Do unto others as you'd have them do unto you', that's the only Judaism I want. You can keep whatever traditions you care to. I won't interfere."

Mother pushed the subject to the back of her mind. What did it matter anyway? She would make him a Jewish home, surround him with Jewish traditions, cook him Jewish food, and make a Jewish man out of him by every means at her disposal. Surely that was what God expected of every young Jewish woman, to be the perfect wife and mother? Who wanted a career? There was great prestige in being the first among your friends to marry. She had so many hopes and dreams. No momentary qualm would undermine her determination to fulfill her calling. This, after all, was her destiny. Without doubt she would inspire in the next generation the faith of her ancestors.

2

I was born in Gateshead shortly after the war, in a place called Felling, notable only for its male voice choir. Gateshead was dismal and depressed in those difficult days and Felling was Gateshead at its greyest. Ration cards were barely in the dustbin when many of the local pits whirred to a standstill and the dole queue more than tripled.

This was where my father bought his first practice. It was all he could afford. Some budding Jewish doctors could look to their parents for financial help and they were only too pleased to give it. After all, they had toiled, scrimped, scrounged, even starved to see their offspring secure in a well-established profession. For a Jew to be an educated, respected member of society, with a contribution to make, was the realisation of a once impossible dream. But with no father to support him my father struggled through college and was thrilled with the great potential of the vast old stone house he had acquired.

It was hardly what my grandparents had had in mind for their daughter. Each of its seventeen rooms was in a state of total disrepair. They surveyed the general dilapidation, swallowed their horror, and tried to kindle some glimmer of enthusiasm in my mother, who had given way to hysterics at first sight. It was a beginning, wasn't it? Everyone has to start somewhere, and standing there in solitary splendour on the top of the hill, looking down on the rows of cobbled streets and smoking chimneys, it did have a certain dignity. Gran rose to the challenge, supervised a total redecoration, ordered carpets and curtains, interviewed maids and gardeners.

"You see what a little imagination can do?" she urged my mother, who went on muttering about the cellars and the rats and the tunnels to the Tyne. "Rats never bother humans," she snapped.

One day father's surgery was brought to a standstill by a blood-curdling scream. Patients in the waiting-room froze with terror. Mother rushed into the examination room, oblivious of what state of undress some poor patient might be in.

"A rat, a rat, there's a rat in the oven," she screamed, "and," she added, as an injured afterthought, "it's licked all the custard out of the custard tart I was making for tea."

"Can't you see how busy I am?" said my father, ushering her out as quickly as possible. "All this fuss for a little mouse." Nonchalantly he swung open the oven door. "You see," he said, then peered in. "Good grief!" he exclaimed, and slammed it shut in a hurry. "It's the size of a cat." They switched on the gas and waited fifteen minutes, but when the oven door was gingerly opened again, the rat had disappeared as mysteriously as it arrived.

From then on the rat-catcher made a courteous, quiet visit once a month, and took away whatever he found in a black suitcase. The rats never bothered me. Their scuffling and scratching was a bit annoying when I was trying to get to sleep, but that was all. Nor were they my mother's only source of misery. She was often lonely and bored. The days were long and dreary.

Felling provided most of the local collieries with manpower, and the manpower with bronchitis, pneumonia and poverty. When my father disappeared into the surgery early in the morning, he rarely emerged before late evening. There was no such thing as an appointment to see the doctor in those days. Sometimes, especially in bad weather, the queue of patients went right round the waiting-room, out of the surgery door and down the street. Mother was unused to so little Jewish company, and despite the kindness of the people, felt uneasy and isolated. If the house was grand by Tyneside's standards, it certainly was by hers. She began to devote her days to making it as perfect as it could be in every way. No picture was ever crooked, no ornament out of place, every curtain fold measured to the last quarter of an inch. Aesthetics lost their meaning. Everything was valued by how easily it could be dusted.

She was not the only one of her generation of Jewish women to succumb to some obsession about her home. It was almost a cultural hazard. Aunt Vera would stand outside her toilet with a duster in her hand whenever it was in use, waiting for it to be vacated so that she could repolish the seat. Her friends and relatives whispered to each other that that was taking cleanliness to its limit. They giggled and went on with their own particular fads.

A certain Jewish cookbook, instruction manual of many a Jewish bride, suggested that the Jewish home was to run as smoothly as a Swiss clock. It was to be swept, dusted, scrubbed and polished daily, as of course were the children, so that the man of the house could return from work to order, serenity and his favourite meal piping hot on the table.

If a young Jewish woman made what was considered to be "a good match" it normally implied her husband could provide her with domestic staff. The problem was that this made her semi-redundant and forced her to create some justification for her existence. The growth of Zionism meant there was always fund-raising to be done, that or making her home more immaculate than everyone else's.

Once the glamour and novelty of being a married lady

wore off my mother lamented her carefree life of dances and parties. Charitable works had no appeal at all. She was twenty and her future seemed frighteningly long and empty. Pregnancy postponed most of her misery. I came first, then seventeen months later my brother David was born, to my disgust I am told. I soon warmed to him and we became inseparable companions as we grew up together in that huge house. Hand in hand we rushed down the endless dark corridors pursued by ghosts, hobgoblins and wicked witches. Behind every curtain, in every cupboard, at the bottom of every staircase was a hidden world, peopled with all kinds of extraordinary beings. Sometimes we tripped over my mother on hands and knees, straightening the curtains we had ruffled on one of our daring voyages of discovery.

At all costs father must not be disturbed, not at breakfast when he opened his post, standing in front of the dining-room fire, not at coffee-time when he and his partners smoked their pipes and laughed together in the study. At lunchtime he was out on his visits, at teatime he was back in the surgery, so we normally ate in the draughty kitchen with the nanny and home-helps around a long, pine kitchen table. The atmosphere depended greatly on the mood and temperament of the adults present and how well they related to one another. Some meals were eaten in oppressive, stony silence. David and I hardly dared look up from our plates. Some were relaxed and happy, others were dominated by the blare of the light programme. One thing was sure, the domestic staff never stayed the same for long. Few could keep up with my mother's extraordinarily high standards and the turnover was rapid. No sooner did I become attached to someone, when she disappeared from my world. It was very unsettling.

Bedtime was always the same. Father popped upstairs between patients in his white coat to tuck us in and say goodnight.

"What shall we have tonight then, kids?"

"Anything but 'Oh Yes, We Have No Bananas' again. Dad."

"Dash it, I've forgotten my ukelele."

"Just tell us a story then."

Whatever we asked for, we always got a cabaret of all-round entertainment. Story after story flowed from the top of his head. He sang us everything from "Your Tiny Hand is Frozen" to "When I'm Cleaning Windows". I knew few nursery rhymes, but could manage an aria or two from Puccini or Verdi. Sadly my mother's loud abuse whenever my father started to sing hid from us how good his voice really was.

We loved Friday evenings. They were special, the Sabbath. My mother and father never went out and David and I were allowed to stay up late and eat with them. Bathed and scrubbed we would sit in silence waiting for father to appear. Mother would rush in, look anxiously at the clock, grumble, then rush out again to see to the potatoes. Minutes later she would be back to check the table, which was set for a banquet. She always scrutinised the silver, her eyes darting from one piece to another.

"Lizzie always misses that patch there, right under the handle." Out of her pocket came the inevitable duster and she would put the home-help's lapse to rights. Sometime after seven the surgery door would slam. There was a pause as father took off his white coat and threw it on to a peg. Then he rushed into the room, donned his skullcap and found the place in the prayer book.

"Is the food spoilt?"

"Is it ever? Isn't it always gefüllte fish on *Shabbas*?"

"I wonder who started that particular tradition? Do you suppose Moses' wife inflicted cold fried fish cakes on him every Friday evening?" Father lifted the lid off a tureen and peered inside. "And salad!"

"Now don't start grumbling. You'll put the children

17

off. I've made it in a dressing just how you like it, especially for you.''

"I don't like salad eith . . ."

David was silenced by one of my mother's terrible stares. She picked up the box of matches, which was the signal that the occasion was about to begin. Slowly, and with great dignity, she lit the Sabbath candles, muttering to herself in Hebrew, a distant look in her eyes. As the tiny flames sprang to life, casting shadows on the wall, giving the room a magic glow, she paused, transfixed, so unlike herself that David and I gazed in wonder. What was she thinking about? We supposed she was praying, but never really knew.

"Vay' erev vay voker yom ha'shishi . . . And it was evening and it was morning, the sixth day . . ."

I loved the lilting, familiar sound of *Kiddush*, the Sabbath prayer. It was a tradition my father took seriously and one of the few pieces of Hebrew he could read with any fluency, because he knew it off by heart. I knew every inflexion of his voice and could say the words quietly with him. I was not sure what they actually meant, for any attempt my father made at reading the translation simultaneously for our benefit was disrupted after the first line by a command from my mother to "stop messing about!" But the gist was that God had made the world in six days, rested on the seventh and that was why we had weekends. It seemed very sensible. If only we did not have to spend it visiting relatives! Maybe mother's brother, uncle Mark, only four years older than I, would take us up to the attic and show us his new records and train set. And aunt Vera might let me rummge through her jewellery and make-up boxes. Or even better, perhaps it would be one of those marvellous Saturdays when mother was too busy to visit the family and father would take us down to the coast, to Whitley Bay.

"David, stand straight and stop lounging!" David and I

jumped at my mother's voice. She had just returned from yet another whirlwind visit to the kitchen.

"Amen," said father wearily, and put the prayer book reverently down. "Perhaps one of these weeks we'll finish without interruption?" He lifted his large silver goblet, waited for mother to slice the *chollah*, the plaited Sabbath loaf, drank, then passed the goblet round so that we could all have a sip. "Good *Shabbas*."

"*Shabbat shalom*."

The festive nature of the occasion suddenly returned. Everyone hugged everyone else. Even my father's non-Jewish partners came in to give us their greetings and get their Sabbath kisses.

When the Sabbath was over, most Saturday evenings my parents went out together. My mother loved dancing and my father indulged her fancy for night-clubs and parties as often as he could. Her sumptuous wardrobe of diaphanous chiffons and glittering sequins was a world of magic for me. Occasionally we saw her in all her splendour, when David and I were summoned to the lounge, a room we never saw by day, and standing in our dressing-gowns were instructed to greet the guests she was entertaining. How we admired her. But when we needed a soft, cosy lap, the home-help had to do.

I should have liked a friend. David was all right, but he was my brother. We drove our trikes to the end of the drive and stared out through the wrought-iron gates at the queue of patients waiting at the surgery door. A huddle of faceless grey figures, a hotch-potch of mackintoshes, caps and headsquares, which never acknowledged our existence. I never knew whether it was because we were the doctor's children or whether they sensed we were somehow different because we were Jews. Mother was always telling us that Jews were different from other people: "They don't dress like we do. They don't eat like we do.

19

They go to churches and have different festivals and traditions."

Sometimes she called them "Christians". At other times, if she was describing behaviour of which she did not particularly approve, she called them "*goyim*", a Yiddish word meaning gentiles. Whatever the reason, our secluded little world was completely separate from the one out there, beyond the six-foot stone walls surrounding our garden.

"Would you like to go exploring?" I asked David one morning, when there was nothing of any particular interest to see through the gate. I was about eight at the time. "I mean, we could always run away."

He looked at me in horror. "We can't. Where would we go? They'd find us and we'd get spanked."

"No we wouldn't. We won't be long. I've seen a park with some swings and a slide in it from the car window. It's only just up that road there."

I tried the gate. It opened. No one was around. We ran up the road at great speed, revelling in the extraordinary sensation of freedom. My only fear was that I could not remember to any degree of accuracy where the park actually was and might not be able to find it, but I was not going to tell that to David. To my great delight, after we had been running for what seemed an age and were just beginning to gasp for breath, some brightly painted swings appeared in the distance. My sense of achievement was complete. Such was my exhilaration that I never noticed the car which suddenly converged upon us until a firm hand on the back of my dress whisked me through the air and deposited me on a car seat. Two minutes later we were once again safely behind the six-foot walls. In fact we were in my father's study receiving a ceremonial thrashing with his slipper. The grand adventure ended in ignominy. Never again did David allow himself to be carried along by my insatiable curiosity.

One Christmas the daily help invited David and I to her house on Boxing Day. It was a damp, chilly afternoon and I slid my hand in hers and huddled close as the iron gate clanged shut behind us and we set off down into the town. In the foggy haze of a winter afternoon each street seemed much like the next, row upon row of terraced houses and nowhere any sign of a tree or a garden. We suddenly turned left into yet another tiny cobbled street and stopped abruptly outside a bottle-green door. She pushed it open and for me it might have been the opening of Pandora's box.

Inside was the brightest, cosiest little world I had ever seen, like something from one of the story books I read. No hall, just this tiny living room with its glowing coal fire and in the corner a vast Christmas tree, shimmering with dozens of coloured balls. I had never seen anything so beautiful before. We huddled round the fire, pulled crackers and ate mince pies.

"One day, I'm going to have a home like this," I told myself, as we went back out into the fog and trudged back up the hill to the big house at the top.

When I was nine years old everything changed. We moved away from the constant ringing of telephone and door-bell into a standard semi in what was regarded as a nice part of Gateshead. Vicky, my sister, was born and I suspect she was something of a surprise. My parents promised to provide her with a companion, but she cried mercilessly night after night for years and in penance had to grow up alone. This time there was no nanny. My mother reminded us continually that a doctor's salary did not stretch as far as it once did. We played in the street with other children and got the bus to school by ourselves.

For this tiny glimpse of normality there was a price to pay. The time had come for us to begin our Hebrew instruction. We had never mixed with other Jewish children, and it worried my mother. She rang the Rabbi who

21

had married her. Of course we could join his *cheder*, his Hebrew school. There was plenty of room in the beginner's class. Only two hours on a Sunday morning. It was enough to start with. What had kept her so long from taking an interest in her children's Jewish education?

"Two hours on a Sunday morning," David groaned. "Do we have to?"

"It does seem a bit much," my father said mildly.

"Oh you, if it depended on you a right pair of little *goyim* we'd have." My mother, like most Jews, interspersed her sentences with Yiddish words when roused. That her children should grow up as *goyim*, with no knowledge of their heritage, was the worst threat she could hold over my father's head. She had given up on him by now. He kept some of the traditions, such as the Sabbath, to keep the peace and because it was part of our family life, but being a Jew was never allowed to interfere with either his professionalism as a doctor or his leisure. My parents had countless arguments over his Saturday morning surgery and afternoon trips to the football match.

"You want me to give up medicine and pedal cheap souvenirs, do you?" he asked mother one day in utter exasperation. The veiled reference to one of her closest friends who had given up his medical studies when he married into a very orthodox family and was prevailed upon to accept a partnership in their china business, finally silenced my mother on that point. But every Jewish mother knows there is a time to put her foot down, and that moment had just arrived.

"I may not be as good a Jew as I would have liked," she said, casting a withering look in my father's direction, "but my children will be!"

One Sunday morning she straightened David's tie and patted the bow on the back of my dress for the umpteenth time, then deposited us on the synagogue steps, dressed up like china dolls in a glass cabinet. We were ushered by the

Rabbi's two daughters into a large airy hall, filled with small groups of children whose chatter died away as the strangers appeared.

"Name? Date of birth?" The dark, ferocious-looking daughter with hairy arms recalled my attention. "Do you know your alphabet?"

"What a stupid question," I thought. "At our age, of course we do." I looked at David. He did not move, and his bright-blue eyes looked enormous. I nodded for both of us.

"Then read me this."

A large book was shoved under my nose filled with the strangest hieroglyphics I had ever seen. I looked up helplessly.

"Then you don't read Hebrew?"

I bit my lip.

"Ah well," she sighed, softening a little, "I don't know what parents are coming to these days. I suppose we must begin at the beginning. Turn the book round, we read from right to left, and let's start with 'aleph'."

Aleph, bet, daled . . . After one lesson I could string two or three consonants together with a couple of vowels; after two lessons I could manage a short Hebrew word, and after five or six a short sentence was quite possible.

"When do they teach you what it means?" I whispered to a fellow student when the teacher's back was turned. His friendly face became a total blank. He shrugged in response. I waited and nothing happened, so I asked the teacher.

"Well, my little one, do you want to run before you can walk? As long as you can read your prayer book what else matters? And then, after all, we are only women, you and I."

I thought of how my mother hated going to the synagogue with my father because he always let her down. She would watch him from the women's gallery, laughing and joking with his friends downstairs, fumbling through the prayer book and digging them in the ribs when he lost the place. Everyone knew that almost everyone else could not translate a word of what they were reading, no matter how fluent it sounded, but they at least read Hebrew well enough not to lose the place. My father never even attempted to hide his unfamiliarity with it all, that was what riled her. A decent show of piety would have kept her happy, but father enjoyed her annoyance much too much for that. She lived in dread of the day the Rabbi would bestow the great honour of inviting him up onto the *bimah*, the raised platform, to read a portion of the law from the silver-encased scrolls. On that day his folly really would be plain for all to see. But I had the sneaking suspicion that should it happen, my father would rise to the occasion as he always did. Besides, our Sabbath attendance was far too spasmodic for that event ever to occur.

"You two had better be good pupils," she said, whenever we complained that Hebrew classes were boring, "or you'll end up like your father."

"Didn't you ever go to *cheder*?" we asked him in wonder.

"Well, your grandmother thought I did," he said with a grin, "but I hardly ever got there. There was more fun to be had on the beach at Redcar with our ukeleles. And then, if I happened to catch your aunt Vera in Notoriani's Ice Cream Parlour with one of her young men, she'd have to buy my silence."

"The beach at Redcar! Notoriani's Ice Cream Parlour! Lucky so-and-so! If I were to truant where would I go? Just my luck to get found out the first time anyway," I thought as I huddled closer to the paraffin heater in the synagogue kitchen, watching the steam rise from my sodden mackintosh. Mr. Rosenberg's class now, that was where being a studious pupil had got me, promotion! Two hours on a Sunday morning was not enough. *Cheder* now

24

devours one hour, three evenings a week as well. My feet squelch in my shoes. I hug my stomach in a vain effort to stifle the inner rumblings. I suppose I could try and do some homework while I wait for the class to start. My fingers are too numb to write. I can hardly see the clock. There seems to be more Tyneside fog in the room than out.

Five o'clock at last! Thank goodness for that—time for prayer drill. Every evening the same! Boys line up at the front facing Israel, girls sit quietly at the desks. The boys are learning to be men. One day they'll wind phylacteries on their arms and foreheads morning and evening and recite the ancient prayers in their homes. Dad doesn't, but uncle Solly does. I've seen him. In fact he likes us to watch him. He sways about muttering to himself and looking holy. It's called *davening*. I wonder if swaying helps you to pray? Mum says uncle Solly has bacon for breakfast after he's said his prayers so God never listens to him anyway. I wonder why he doesn't listen to women either. It seems a bit unfair. Bet I could *daven* as well as any of the boys.

"Sir," said Peter, an outsized boy, who was obviously squeezed into his short trousers every morning and ballooned out of every exit, "are you sure Israel's in this direction?" He was staring at some graffiti on the beige gloss wall until he was cross-eyed.

"Pity," he continued, no response forthcoming, "if it was over in that direction we could face the window."

Mr. Rosenbery looked up and caught sight of the huge piece of pink bubble-gum which bloated the boy's mouth. He watched it revolving round and round as if it were his washing at the launderette, opened his mouth, but said nothing. Either he was mesmerised, or, noticing the tie flung over one shoulder and the skullcap hanging limply over one ear, decided not to take on yet another hopeless case. "Continue your praying," he snapped.

As Peter turned back to the wall his eyes met mine. He rolled them to the ceiling, made a strange gobbling sound, then, his back to me, began to rock backwards and forwards. The pages of his prayer book flicked over at an unbelievable speed. Two minutes later, which was the record in our class for a passage in the prayer book which normally takes about fifteen minutes to recite, he stopped instantly, then walked back to his seat with a grin.

"Not bad, eh?" he asked, looking over in my direction. "I can pray like the Rabbi's son too!"

"Open your books at page twenty and we will begin our translation. Abraham, if you remember, is journeying through the wilderness."

"Not still, sir. He was doing that last week. In fact, he was doing that last year." With a self-congratulatory smile, Alan, whose ears stuck horizontally out from his head and served as hinges for his school cap, looked round for our approval. He was always in trouble. I lost count of the times that the broad grin which stretched the whole breadth of his face would be wiped out by a sudden violent slap, when Mr. Rosenberg's patience was strained beyond all endurance. The cocky little lad would break out into the most nerve-grating howling, and Mr. Rosenberg, embarrassed by his sudden lack of control, and even more by the terrible din, would cover him in kisses.

"Ugh," he said one day, wiping his face with the corner of his sleeve, "I think I'd rather have his slaps."

Mr. Rosenberg was reputed to be the most learned Jewish scholar in the North East. If he was, it was wasted on us. We thought him the oldest man alive, and he was about forty-five at the time. Everything about him was bird-like: his little beak of a nose and balding round head, the grey goatee beard resting on his swollen chest, the tiny, beady, black eyes peering at you through bottle-bottom spectacles which periodically slipped down his nose and were lifted by a sudden facial contortion, so that

26

you never knew if he held you in utter disdain, or had just smelled a rather nasty smell.

"Malchah, continue translating." Malchah was my Hebrew name after my pious great-great-grandmother, but half the girls in the class were Malchah too. It struck me that Jewish parents must have been a bit hard-pressed to find Hebrew names for their daughters. "Boys, listen to Malchah. Her translation is always faultless."

"Little squirt," murmured Peter, to my immense satisfaction. Only I knew that I could not translate a single word. Mr. Rosenberg read the translation at the beginning of the class, and, having a reasonable memory, I simply learnt it parrot-fashion.

The boredom of such an exercise was excruciating. Any avenue of escape was worth a try.

"Please, Sir, can I be excused?"

"You, Malchah? I'm surprised, but of course."

I ran upstairs, savouring every minute of freedom, dawdling as long as I dared, then ambled nonchalantly back into the classroom.

"And the blessing?" Mr. Rosenberg's words halted me in my track back to my desk.

"Blessing, Sir?"

"Yes, blessing, the one for after . . . ! You may come to the front of the class and read it for us all." In Judaism there is a blessing for every occasion, a journey, a visit, fruit from the ground, fruit from the tree. Mr. Rosenberg made sure we knew them all, but up until that moment that particular one had escaped my notice. It seemed to me to be the longest in the prayer book. There had to be other ways of killing time.

"Please, Sir, tell us a Bible story."

"Please, Sir, why do Jewish boys have to have that operation, you know?"

"Please, Sir, who was Jesus Christ?" To my horror the room went deadly silent. What had I said? Why was

27

everyone looking at me? "P-p-please, Sir," I stammered, "it was only that the girls at school tell me that I killed him, so I was just wondering . . ."

Mr. Rosenberg seemed to swell before my very eyes and I thought he was going to burst. I had never seen such anger before.

"Never," he hissed, "never let me hear that name on the lips of a Jewish girl."

I sat down. Mr. Rosenberg cleared his throat and the class continued in an uncomfortable sort of a way.

I had a fascination for God and continued to afflict Mr. Rosenberg with my endless questioning. The trouble was I do not think he could distinguish genuine searching from the distraction technique we all employed. And so I never received a satisfactory answer.

"Why must we always say the right blessing for everything?"

"Because the essence of Judaism is to show our constant devotion to God."

"But Sir, what if you don't know whether the fruit grows on a tree or in the ground, how can you say the right blessing then?" Alan butted in and waited for the laughter. He always spoilt things.

"But," I continued, desperately trying to regain Mr. Rosenberg's attention, "how do we please God?"

"You learn the Torah, Malchah, the five books of Moses, the laws of our people, and you keep them."

"Five books? But Sir, we still haven't finished the first one. We'll never get there."

"You worry too much . . . for a girl."

One day Mr. Rosenberg asked me to stay behind after the end of the class. "Malchah," he said, wrinkling up his nose so that he could peer at me more closely through his spectacles, "I have a great privilege for you. Since your translation is so faultless, since you have such a desire to learn, you shall be the first girl to study for my Torah Diploma.''

"Oh, er, thank you, Sir," I muttered and backed out of the room. I could hardly refuse. What had I let myself in for?

I need not have worried. I soon discovered that the Diploma involved a written rather than a verbal examination of our Hebrew translation, no more than that. While the rest of the class continued to appall Mr. Rosenberg with their ignorance, I was sent into the next room with the Rabbi's son to transcribe on to paper what was recorded on the tape in my head. Within twenty minutes I marched back into the classroom and proudly presented Mr. Rosenberg with my work. He scanned the page, making all kinds of unintelligible grunting noises. Suddenly they stopped and then he gasped, "Malchah what have you done?"

I peered at my paper over his shoulder. What had I done?

"There," he whispered in horror, "look there."

I followed the long bony finger and read, "G.o.d. God. It says God."

"I know what it says. Please do not add to your shame by letting that word pass your lips. Never, except in the most earnest prayer do we use the name of the Holy One, blessed be he."

"Oh I see. That's why when we read the Scriptures we call him '*Ha'shem*', the Name, rather than . . ."

"Of course," Mr. Rosenberg snapped, interrupting me before I could say the inevitable "*Adonai*." "Nor dare we write it in full in English."

I watched him take a tiny penknife from his jacket pocket and cut a square out of the paper all round the letter "o".

"In future you will write G dash d. Do you understand?"

I nodded and wandered to a seat, dumb with amazement. Did God mind what we called him? Did he really require such a pointless exercise?

Somehow Mother discovered that Mr. Rosenberg lived quite near us and it was only polite to offer him a lift to and from the *cheder* on Sunday mornings. David and I were hardly pleased. As if it was not bad enough having him in the car for what seemed an endless quarter of an hour, father would keep up a constant banter on religious matters. We could tell from Mr. Rosenberg's rather uncomfortable shuffle and the fixed smile on his face that he did not quite share father's sense of humour, but could not be rude because he was getting a lift. He must have known my father was not a very religious Jew, but I desperately hoped he would not see how bad he really was. Sometimes I thought father set out to shock him deliberately and was almost under the back seat with embarrassment when we drove up to Mr. Rosenberg's gate.

One day his wife was waiting to meet him. I was staggered. She was dainty and pretty and looked young enough to be his daughter.

"Oh, mum," I said when we arrived home, "you should see Mr. Rosenberg's wife. She's so pretty and has lovely red hair."

Mother smiled. "She may do, I suppose."

"May do? What do you mean?"

"Her hair is not her own. She wears a *sheitel*, a wig. When very orthodox women marry they shave their heads, then keep them covered for the rest of their lives."

I could hardly take it in.

Mother looked at my horror-stricken face then laughed. "And her marriage will have been arranged for her. A learned man is considered a good catch amongst the ultra-orthodox."

Any pretensions I might have had to becoming a more orthodox Jew evaporated in that instant. God could ask too much.

With immense relief I left Hebrew classes after three years, with a Diploma for fluent Hebrew reading, a Diploma in knowledge of the Torah, and a whole load of unanswered questions. David was not so lucky! He had a *Bar Mitzvah* to come. It would be the most important moment of his life, when, in the eyes of the entire Jewish community, he would become a man. On that day, when he stood up in the synagogue before all his aunts, uncles, cousins, and distant relatives, to sing a portion of the Torah, he had to be word perfect, an immense undertaking for a thirteen-year-old.

Individual Hebrew instruction was the only concession to his having any importance on the occasion at all. Mother had been rushing around frantically for months, arranging caterers for a Sabbath luncheon, choosing menus and finding a band for a Sunday afternoon tea dance, trying desperately to kindle some interest in my father, who only reacted when he saw the caterer's estimate.

"What am I, Rothschild? With two daughters to see wed, and you want two hundred at a *Bar Mitzvah* tea party? Where do you find so many relatives? All yours, you realise? Hitler put paid to most of mine."

"Some of the ones that survive are bad enough."

"Yours are so wonderful?"

"Shut up and pass me the seating plan. Now we can't have uncle Solly and uncle Myer at the same table. Everyone knows they haven't been speaking for years. Oh, by the way, there's a bill in the post from Books Fashion House. Well, you do have a wife and two daughters to clothe, and after all, it's father's cousins' business, so we do get a good discount."

Mother liked to keep her money in the family, and the family liked to keep it there too! We had barely opened the dress shop door, when half a dozen harpies swooped on her and carried her off to the model gowns department. I wandered round on my own, fingering the rows of satin and lace, when suddenly I noticed the dress of my dreams. It was a frothy, frilly creation in royal blue chiffon, just like the dress worn by Snow White in Walt Disney's film. I had never worn frills before. Mother preferred to hide my ever-increasing puppy fat in what she called "something tailored", usually beige and ugly. I took the dress down from the rail and got it on as quickly as I could, then rushed to find mother who, clad only in bra and corset, was shouting instructions to the entire department.

"Well, mum?" I said, and twirled round, waiting for her approval. "Isn't this just it?"

She stopped in mid-sentence and glanced in my direction. "It's a bit revealing, isn't it?"

"Not really. It's just that I'm a bit high-busted."

"She has got a lovely figure for her age," said one of the harpies, suddenly aware of a possible sale in another direction.

"You mean she's got a big bust?" my mother shouted from somewhere within a sequinned tube. "Well, you should know. It's your side of the family she gets it from. No, I can't have you looking like a barmaid."

Eventually I persuaded her to let me have a bit cut off the hem and sewn across the offending cleavage, and by the time we went home, leaving garments strewn all over the shop, everyone was happy.

As the great day approached, presents began to arrive in a steady stream. Five writing cases, seven alarm clocks, nine fountain pens. They all had to be laid out for the guests to see, without auntie Sadie noticing that her present was an inferior version of auntie Hilda's. In our more modest house, space provided something of a problem. But for a *Bar Mitzvah* all things were possible. The official photographer, the arranger of plastic flowers, relations, waitresses, caterers with vast tureens of chopped liver and chopped herring which they mixed by hand, all fought their way into every available corner. David and I goggled. We had never seen anyone elbow-deep in chopped liver before. Somehow I could not manage to eat any at the buffet.

"What a big girl you're getting, so like her mummy."

There it went again, a refrain heard so many times that day that I was tempted to join in.

"Soon there'll be a boyfriend and then, please God, a wedding. That will be the next family do. Nothing like a *simcha* for bringing the family together."

"She's time enough," father answered for me, to my great relief, thinking of his bank balance.

David, scrubbed and cropped, in a suit for the first time, wore a vague expression of disbelief, as if everything seemed to be happening to someone else. Like a wooden soldier he stuck out an arm to greet his guests, escorted his mother out for the first dance and read his after-dinner speech.

"I would like to thank my wonderful parents for all they have done for me." Mother had written it! Never mind, she still sat behind a valium-induced haze and lapped up the applause.

I felt sick inside, but why on earth should I? There were relatives here I had not seen for years, some from Israel I had never seen before. This was David's big day and I hated every minute of it. What was it all for, the effort, the expense? David would be the same tomorrow as he was today. There were some things about our religion I really did not understand. One thing was sure. No one else seemed to feel the same. They were all having a good time. Something must be wrong with me. I put it out of my mind, too frightened to delve any deeper.

3

Jewish daughters are supposed to learn all they really
need to know, not from classes, but from their mothers.
And what else does a Jewish daughter need to know except
how to get herself a good catch and keep him happy?

"Your father's not a wealthy man," my mother said
with a regretful shake of the head. "There's not much of a
dowry for you. You'll have to get by on your cooking."

If all her hard work and effort had been amply rewarded, I should have married a Rothschild at least. By
the time I was fourteen there was nothing I did not know
about Jewish cuisine and keeping a kosher kitchen.

"Stand here and watch . . . Stir this . . . beat that . . .
How many times have you salted the meat? Do it again.
There must be no trace of blood in the rinsing water . . .
Make the Yorkshire Puddings—with water, not milk . . .
No, we can't have cheese sauce. How many times must I
tell you, we can't mix meat and dairy produce?"

In interpreting the law which said, "Thou shalt not boil
a kid in its mother's milk," my mother never went to the
lengths which some of her friends did—separate dishes for
milk and meat, separate sinks, separate towels, separate
dish washers, if you could rise to it—but nevertheless she
refused to serve the two together at a meal. She insisted

her kitchen should be kosher and only bought her meat from a kosher butcher.

"Why bother?" my father murmured, whenever she complained about the price of kosher meat, "there's only one way to slit an animal's throat and let the blood drain out, whoever the slaughterer is."

Yet mother persisted in the belief that every Jewish man would only know true peace of mind when he was sure his wife kept a strictly kosher kitchen and would serve him gefüllte fish on the Sabbath. The latter was an unwritten law. Great-grandma always served it on *Shabbas*. So did grandma. So, inevitably, did mother. And since our washing was always hung to dry on a rack hanging from the kitchen ceiling, it was just as inevitable that we would go to school on Monday morning smelling like chopped, fried fish balls.

Yiddishkeit, not Judaism, that was what really mattered to my mother and her friends. You could be as ignorant about your religion as you chose, reject whatever ritual you found tiresome, never attend the synagogue, as long as you had that elusive, indescribable feel for the Jewish way of life. Tradition mattered more than piety. All that was required of a good Jewess was to pass on to her daughters the ability to create a real Jewish home, just as it had been for generations. Here was the key to the stability of the Jewish family and the survival of the race.

"Ah, but there is something very special about the Jewish home," or that is what I am always told. So many non-Jewish people revere and romanticise it that I am sure they know something I do not. And so many Jews succumb to its extraordinary influence, that no matter how old they are, or how far away, they are inextricably bound to it by a thousand emotional threads. How can I explain it? Our home was not exactly average, but nor was it untypical. "We don't do that, we're Jewish," was a refrain I heard many times. I did not want to be different. I wanted to be just like my friends, but somehow being Jewish did make me feel special. That was what home gave to me, a sense of destiny, despite the frustrations the feeling that it was rather a privilege to be a Jew, and not just an embarrassing freak of birth. After all, if Hitler had had his way, so I was told, or the many other tyrants and nations who had tried to get rid of my ancestors, I would not have existed at all. I was one of a chosen people, chosen by whom and for what I could not understand, but that did not worry me at first. We had our own festivals and celebrations which none of my schoolfriends knew anything about. They belonged to us and were a secret bond between us, linking us to each other and every Jew, near or far, long since dead, or yet to come.

The only Christian festival for which I envied my schoolfriends was Christmas. The rest seemed terribly dull. I would have loved a Christmas tree of my own, dripping with shimmering baubles, and fairy lights twinkling round the front door. Mother bought a kosher turkey, since the occasion was technically a bank holiday, but I was sure it was not quite the same as having crackers and decorations. Then, everyone shared in Christmas; we had parties and a tree at school. So perhaps our festivals were more magic after all.

David and I were at a great disadvantage when it came to understanding what they all meant. Mr. Rosenberg reckoned mother would explain them, but mother never could remember which was which, or why she was doing what.

"What's this one about, mum?" we asked her one December, grinning at one another, as she lit her *menorah*, the nine-branched candelabra, checking that each of the tiny candles was absolutely vertical, so that no wax could drip on the brass and ruin the display.

"Er, Esther," she said vaguely.

"Wrong," we shouted triumphantly.

"Something to do with the temple?" she asked hopefully.

36

"Yes," we prompted.

"Somebody's oil lasted eight days."

"Whose?"

"Elijah's?"

We looked unconvinced. "Does Judas Maccabeus ring a bell?"

No glimmer of recognition passed her face.

"Mum, *Chanukah*, the Feast of Lights is all about his heroic defence of the temple. His tiny drop of oil lasted eight days. It was a miracle."

"Well, whoever it was I wish he'd never started this business, because now we have to do it every year."

Mother regarded most of the major Jewish holy days as an affliction to be endured. She carried out the traditions as if the appeasement of God's wrath depended on it; not because it gave her any real sense of spiritual comfort, but because that was the way things had always been done in her family. The arrival of September filled her with dismay.

"Three Jewish holidays, three in four weeks, and I haven't started to think, cook, clean or anything."

Rosh Hashanah, the New Year, is the first of the three and supposed to be one of the most important occasions. Dressed up in our new finery David and I would sit in the synagogue waiting with great anticipation for the weird sound of the ram's-horn. Producing any sound at all on the *shofar* is no mean achievement. I have witnessed very few convincing performances. One New Year the Rabbi blew so hard he turned purple and we thought he was bound to collapse, but still nothing happened. Steadying his hat, and summoning every ounce of dignity he possessed, he drew his breath, then gave the thing everything he had got. Out came a shrill, cracked little squeak. The respectful silence was suddenly shattered by the raucous laughter of a child, who could not hold it in any longer. I was glad it was not me. The Rabbi removed the ram's-horn from his mouth and fixed the young renegade with a stare, which instantly turned him to stone. We all watched for a further quarter of an hour, twiddled our thumbs, stared at the ceiling, coughed politely behind our prayer books, but the instrument refused to cooperate, so no joyous sound heralded that *Rosh Hashanah*.

Some time during the following week, like most other Jews, we paid our annual visit to the family graves. It struck me as an awfully morbid and boring prelude to *Yom Kippur*, the Day of Atonement. Everyone stood around looking so sheepish. Flowers are never left on Jewish graves, so no one seemed to know what to do with their feelings. They rubbed the gravel with the toes of their shoes, read and re-read the inscriptions on the stone slabs, as if they might have changed since last year.

"Do you think we used the right wording, dear?"

"Have they been dead that long, God rest their souls? Where do the years go?"

When we were small, we sat in the car outside the cemetery and waited. The adults emerged looking very serious and blinking.

"What did you do, dad?"

"I said a prayer."

We had driven fifty miles to Teesside, dragged the local Rabbi away from his fireside chair on a Sunday afternoon, had hung around for what seemed an eternity on a biting autumnal day.

"Couldn't you have said it at home?"

"Yes."

No explanation! There never was. That was something I never grew up to accept.

Yom Kippur is the most solemn occasion in the Jewish calendar. It is one of several fast days, but the only one my mother insisted we keep. Once I was twelve no sip of water was to pass my lips from sundown to sundown. It is supposed to be a day for confessing one's sins to God and making New Year's resolutions. I found it hard in my early teens to know exactly what my sins were, so I went to the synagogue for light relief, rather than the right religious reasons. On fast days there had to be compensations. There was nothing to pass the time at home.

"Who do you think will be the first to faint and be carried out this year, David?"

"I bet it's Peter again."

"He just does it to show off."

"All right then, how much do you bet?"

We waited with ghoulish anticipation for the first victim of hunger to crumple into a heap. Last year it was a man, it usually was, and we women had a bird's eye view from the upstairs gallery. You knew when it happened. Everything went quiet. Even gran stopped moaning for a cup of tea. Then the service was resumed with more chatter, shuffling, yawning, stretching and tummy-rumbling than ever.

One part of the service always enthralled me. The chatter died down, the children stopped whizzing their Dinky toys around the wooden seats and an awed hush descended on the congregation. Several of the men downstairs, the *cohanim*, or priests, covered their heads with their prayer shawls and, swaying in harmony, chanted a blessing on the people just like the priests in the temple of old. No one was supposed to look, but I was fascinated by the haunting sound and uncanny sight of all those writhing pieces of white satin beneath us.

From that moment on, the ladies' gallery began to empty. One mother after another was lured away to her kitchen by overpowering thoughts of roast chicken, chopped herring, luscious desserts and all the ritual preparations for breaking the fast. Food always tasted marvellous on that night. It was amazing how much you could put away, once your tummy had been cajoled into coping with the onslaught by a glass of milk and soda water. What would it be tonight? The drooling anticipation became almost unbearable until at last the ram's-horn put us all out of our misery and the synagogue emptied as it never did on any other day. Why linger to chat when there would be food on the table?

Succoth, the Feast of Booths or Harvest, came just after the New Year and the Day of Atonement and suffered for it. By that time it was very difficult to take yet more holiday from work and school, so it more or less passed us by at home.

"Dad, build us a booth in the garden."

"A what?"

"Well, a kind of wooden shed will do. All Jews are supposed to have them."

David and I envisaged moving into it for eight days, the duration of the festival, with sleeping bags and pyjamas to spend several nights under the stars.

"Your father, build a shed! Are you crazy? He can barely even change a plug!"

We looked from mother to father, hoping he would defy her words, but no luck. We would have to be satisfied with what *cheder* would do for us. They marched us out, one class at a time, into a rickety, makeshift contraption in the grounds, which looked as if it might collapse if we sneezed. Branches and twigs with bits of plastic fruit and flowers attached to them hung down from above and threatened to throttle you if you did not watch your step. Mr. Rosenberg, his little chest puffed out until he looked as plump and round as a well-fed robin, presented each of us with a glass of lemonade and a plain biscuit. The proper blessings said, we were allowed to indulge. We kept our eyes on the lemonade as long as we could, then someone looked up and we all had to hide our helpless, ungrateful giggling behind the plastic greenery.

Mother only insisted we attend the synagogue on major festivals, but since she rarely came with us, even that seemed a bit much at times. One festival was too good to be missed, however—*Purim*, the feast of Esther. The syn-

40

agogue was quite noisy on most occasions, with people coming and going and kissing their relatives as they came or went, but the Rabbi only stopped the service when he could no longer hear what he was saying himself. He would rest his elbows on the pulpit and, tapping his foot with a look of mock weariness on his face, stare at the women's gallery, where most of the noise was coming from, until the realisation dawned that the service had come to a standstill and a temporary, penitent silence would descend. But at *Purim* the more noise the better. As the Rabbi recounted the famous story of Esther, we booed with all our might every time the name Haman was mentioned, and cheered loudly for Esther and Mordecai. *Cheder* once inflicted a *Purim* play on the parents. Mr. Rosenberg gave me permission to join another class for the great event. I was so excited. Stardom at last! And then I realised I was only wanted as a walk-on extra, a Babylonian soldier. They are not even mentioned in the story.

Of all the festivals, the Passover was the favourite. It made the others seem almost insignificant. Eight days without cake, biscuits or cornflakes, eight days craving for things you never normally ate, eight days of mother complaining of chronic constipation—I cannot think why I liked the Passover at all, except that the first two nights, known as the *Seder* or "service" nights, made up for everything. Everybody had to be there, gran, grandpa, aunts, uncles, the whole family came together to celebrate the deliverance of our people from slavery in Egypt three thousand years ago.

Every year followed an invariable pattern. That was part of the fun. You knew exactly what was coming.

"We can't start, we can't start," panted gran, as she opened the front door. She was back in the kitchen before we were over the front doorstep.

"The meringue isn't risen and Mark's in the bath."

"He would be, of course," exploded my mother. "You

get out of there, and quick," she yelled, in the direction of the raucous singing.

"All right, dearest sister," the reply mimicked her voice exactly.

"And stop the racket!"

"Just practising for the occasion, you know."

The sound of laughter and splashing and scale singing continued. Mother shrugged her shoulders and made for the nearest armchair.

"Let me sit down. What a week! I couldn't stand that again. I'm worn out."

She flopped down in the armchair next to grandpa's. He was hunched, as he always was, over the two-bar electric fire, trying to achieve what his circulation no longer could and put some feeling of warmth into his hands.

"Uh-huh," was all he ever said, but it was enough for his daughter.

"The price of the Passover food this year. And no one ever has everything you want. I went to Cohen's for cheese, and Steinberg's for chocolate, and Bloom's for orange squash."

David, fired by the thought of the huge cardboard box, packed to the brim with jars, boxes, packets and tins, which had been deposited on our doorstep during the week, suddenly said, "I thought you could eat anything which didn't have something in it to make it rise."

"Right," I said, knowingly, "we can't eat leaven."

David was silent, then he said, "Does cheese have leaven in it, or squash, or jam?"

Father, at the other end of the room, looked up at us over the top of the *Evening News*. "No, they don't," he said, with a sideways glance at my mother, "but at Passover time you can only buy them from shops where they have the special 'kosher for Passover' label."

"That means the Rabbi has watched it being made and

42

blessed it," said David, incredulously, "so what difference does that make?"

"A great deal, it doubles the price!"

Father had very little time for the *Beth Din*'s system of sanctioning kosher food. "The Death Bin", he called it. "They'd sanction anything at a price."

"Now Manny," Gran paused at the door, half-way back to the kitchen, "you know we have to do things properly. I've always expected it of my daughter." Father disappeared behind the newspaper. "And incidentally," she said, looking at mother, "you have soaked the glassware, haven't you?"

"Yes, mam."

"And changed over to the Passover set of crockery?"

"Yes, mam."

"And checked every corner for the tiniest breadcrumbs?"

"Why do you think I'm so exhausted?"

I could not help but smile. One tradition we dispensed with in our house was the father's torchlight search, followed by his children, for any bit of leaven which may have escaped the spring-cleaning. Father regarded it as a futile exercise, since no self-respecting breadcrumb would ever dare defy the daily help's vacuum cleaner or my mother's meticulous inspection.

"Good evening, everybody," Mark appeared, ruddy and polished. "A kiss from the children, and then we'll begin."

"About time," mother scowled, resenting the way her younger brother always controlled the evening's events.

We made our way to the table, and what a table it was! The cloth was bleached until it dazzled and crinkled when you moved up against it. The best silver had been polished until you could see your own reflection quite clearly. Each person had a tiny silver wine goblet, which shimmered in the candlelight. An embroidered coverlet, draped over three pieces of unleavened bread, added a startling dash of scarlet and sapphire. David and I took our places, wide-eyed and open-mouthed.

"What's that for?" asked David, pointing at an egg with a burn mark on its shell, lying on the dish of Passover symbols in the middle of the table. We were so used to seeing these peculiarities every year that it was some time before we looked at them and realised we did not have a clue what they meant. Even if an explanation had been given we always forgot it in the twelve intervening months.

"That symbolises the temple which was destroyed many years ago. Some rabbis think it speaks of hope and new life too," explained Mark.

"And what's that?" David was pointing at the bone which lay next to it.

"That represents the lamb which used to be sacrificed for our sins in the temple at Passover-time. And of course the lambs whose blood was daubed on the doorposts of the homes of the children of Israel."

"And what's this?" David picked up a piece of parsley.

"That reminds us of the hyssop which daubed the blood on."

"And this?"

"David, do be quiet and wait," snapped mother. "Where are the *Haggadah*s?" She looked on the sideboard for the books with the evening's service in them, but Mark was already handing them out.

"Don't give me that one, I had it last year and the print is far too small."

"Who has mine, the one with the wine stain on page fifty-two?"

"Someone scribbled in this one last year."

"I want the one with the colour pictures of the plagues."

"Damn, I've forgotten my reading glasses." Father fumbled in his pockets.

Mother groaned. "Will somebody please start."

44

"All right then, David, off you go," said Mark, "ask the four questions."

"Which four?" said David.

He knew very well which four. In fact this was his moment of glory, when everyone's attention is focused on the youngest male child, whose questions form the basis for the whole evening service. But he could not resist bantering with uncle Mark.

"Any four you like," Mark replied.

We opened our *Haggadahs*, the appropriate opening blessings were made, gran lit the candles, then David read out the famous four questions:

"Why is this night different from all other nights and why do we eat unleavened bread?"

"Why do we eat bitter herbs instead of vegetables?"

"Why do we dip in the dish twice?"

"Why do we eat leaning?"

"And why do you ask the same questions every year?" grinned Mark, "because you always get the same answer."

Grandpa began to read the long, learned, rabbinic explanation from the *Haggadah*. The word "Haggadah" means "telling", because it tells the story of our flight from Egypt, but I never could remember what all the answers were. He got slower and slower until his words were strung together in one loud snore. I was never sure whether the cushions my grandmother put on his chair to prop him up were an attempt to pretend he was leaning, or a last valiant effort to keep him awake.

"For goodness sake take over," gran shouted at Mark, "or we'll be here all night."

"Not yet, he's not quite asleep."

"Ooh look!" David exclaimed, holding up his *Haggadah*. "Look at this picture of the Egyptian soldiers in the middle of the Red Sea. If I pull this tab, see, the waters roll back over them, and they're all drowned."

"Gruesome little beggar, isn't he?" Mark said, staring at the pictures with fascination.

There was another snore from the head of the table and then uncle Mark began to sing—in perfect Hebrew. I could hear Mr. Rosenberg's voice: "Your uncle Mark, how he sings, what diction, what delivery, what pronunciation! He sings in a way I rarely hear today, just like the *Chasidim*, the orthodox of the orthodox, the most beautiful there is."

He did have a marvellous voice. You could not help but be impressed. Gran looked at him, one moment full of fond admiration, and the next filled with acute aggravation, as he stopped mid-flow to discuss the latest progress of Newcastle United with my father.

"Continue," she snapped, and when he did she continued her conversation with my mother behind their *Haggadah*s.

"What a terrible time we had in Egypt," murmured grandpa. Everyone looked up in surprise. "Such things we had to endure." Strangely enough, it did seem as if it all happened yesterday.

My father suddenly started giggling like a naughty schoolboy. Mark's teasing always had that effect on him. He caught gran's eye, cleared his throat, then muttered, "We were slaves in Egypt . . ."

"Manny," said gran, with an air of injured dignity, "you aren't by any chance reading the English translation are you? We don't do that in this house. We're Orthodox, not Reform, here."

I knew father had attended the new Reform Synagogue in Newcastle once or twice to see what it was like. Their services were half in English and they only kept the basic Jewish traditions. That appealed to him. He had tried to hide his recent interest but nothing escaped his mother-in-law.

"Dreadful wine this," mother chipped in, "whoever trod on this lot forgot to wash his feet."

"Well, drink up your second cup, sister dear, because then there's a treat in store."

It was time for the bitter herbs. Grandpa came to with a grunt, saw everyone staring at the Passover dish and picked up the large piece of horseradish root. He shaved off miniature matchsticks and passed them round. I kept passing them on until I ended up with the tiniest sliver.

"You're supposed to be able to taste it," gran said, peering at the tiny speck on my palm, "and it isn't meant to taste nice. It's to remind you of all your ancestors suffered in Egypt."

Everyone dipped their horseradish into a bowl of grey mess called *charoseth*. Ugh! It was made of good things like wine, apples, and walnuts, but it was meant to be the mortar the Israelites used and to me that was exactly how it tasted.

Then we ate a sandwich of horseradish and *charoseth* between two small pieces of *matzo*. That was supposed to be one of the bricks the children of Israel had made. No wonder it seemed to grandpa as if the exodus happened last year.

Only one more endurance test before the meal, a bowl of hard-boiled egg floating in salt water, the eyes and tears of my ancestors. I had to concentrate on keeping it down. I could not bear egg in any form. From now on grandpa had to be watched. He drew out the middle piece of the three pieces of matzo under the coverlet and broke it in half. One half was the *Afikomen*, symbol of the Passover lamb. Grandpa was supposed to hide it and we had to find it and sell it back to him.

We gobbled down an enormous meal, chopped liver pate, chicken soup, roast chicken, a sweet stew called *tsimmes*, then fruit and meringues, coconut haystacks and cinnamon cookies, never once taking our eyes off grandpa.

"Have you hidden it yet, grandpa?"

"Yes."

"Not like last year, when you forgot where you'd put it until mum sat on it, and a fat lot of good it was then!"

We jumped down from our chairs and tore round the house, searching behind every curtain and in every drawer. Mark watched in amusement.

"Here it is," shouted David, triumphantly waving the piece of matzo in the air.

"Decoy!" shouted grandpa and produced five identical pieces from different corners of the room.

"Come on, grandpa, this is the real one. Fifteen shillings split three ways, between David and me and the baby!"

"I don't want it this year."

"But you have to want it."

"What for?"

"It's . . . it's a tradition."

Eventually the teasing stopped and mother secured us a reasonable deal. We gathered again around the table and grandpa took the *Afikomen*, broke it, blessed it, and passed it around. No more food must touch our lips that night. Then he took up the third cup of wine and we all drank. Gran went to the front door and opened it for Elijah. David and I stood with bated breath. Would he come this year to drink his goblet of wine and tell us the Messiah was coming? No, he never did. Every year we were disappointed, all except my father, who drank his wine for him in his absence. It did just occur to me that if he came, he would not be able to stand after he had done his first street, but I imagined that like Santa Claus he had ways and means of overcoming such difficulties.

Grandpa prayed for God's anger to come upon the nations that did not believe in him, and then we drank. Somehow father managed to launch his goblet across the table with the corner of his *Haggadah*. Mesmerised, we all watched the steadily expanding red pool on the table, until gran, realising the service had come to a standstill, looked up and rushed out for a cloth.

"Manny, you get the laundry bill this year."

"But mam," my mother said, to our amazement rising to father's defence, "he didn't stand a chance. We've knocked the goblets down so many times that their stems are all bent, and they don't stand up straight any more."

"And whose fault is that?"

"Well," mother continued, taking a calculated risk, "it was you who knocked the wine over last year, if you remember?"

Gran paused. "Mark, get singing!"

"And a happy *Pesach* to all," grinned Mark. "It isn't a real *Pesach* until someone spills the wine."

He began to sing the traditional folk songs, faster and faster, until David and I gave up altogether. Gran sang different tunes, the ones she sang as a girl. Father, the only one with a real voice, could not follow the Hebrew. The racket rose to a crescendo during "The Kid Sold for Two Farthings", until suddenly it was all over, and the books slammed shut for another year.

"Next year in Jerusalem."

"And please God, may British Airways reduce the fare."

4

My secular education was by courtesy of the Church of England. There was no Jewish day school in existence then and even if there had been my parents would have dismissed the idea as "too narrow". They wanted their children to mix easily in the society and culture of the country of their birth, and attend good private schools with reputations for academic success. In my case the Newcastle Church High School seemed to fulfill the necessary requirements. Most of my Jewish acquaintances at *cheder* attended the Roman Catholic Convent School. Their parents thought another minority religious group would have more sympathy for Jews, but mother had a horror of dark and gloomy convents with their weird religious symbols plastered all over the walls and she hated the idea of my being taught by all those nuns. Besides, she had attended the Sunderland Church High School as a girl—and survived. It had been her only chance to mix with non-Jews, but since there had been three other Jewish girls in her class it had hardly been necessary.

"I had a form teacher," she told me, as she laid out my clothing for my first morning in the senior school, checking to see that everything had been safely labelled with my name, "who used to say to us, 'In recent years the Jewish people have shown themselves to have a remarkable brilliance. It is of the utmost disappointment to me that I happen to have four exceptions in my class.' ''

''Didn't you do very well then?''

''We were always in trouble for chattering and giggling usually. Well, what was the point of studying? You don't need to pass exams to get married and have babies, do you? Still, times have changed. You have chances I never had.''

If the Sunderland Church High School did little for my mother academically, at least it accepted her religion, albeit grudgingly. Any hint of anti-semitism was carefully disguised.

''The Church of England is so tolerant. They understand about Jews,'' she said.

I set off on that first morning with her words ringing in my ears: ''If they get on to anything religious, say you're Jewish and opt out.'' The assembly bell rang. The classroom emptied in a moment, and I was left sitting at my new desk, a carved-on, rickety old thing, the only one left when the other girls had finished choosing theirs. I was obviously the only Jew in my class. The teacher went on marking her register. I wriggled and the desk creaked. She looked up, and, seeing me, frowned.

''Well? Why didn't you follow the others?''

''I'm . . . Jewish.''

''Well, don't just sit there. Jewish prayers, third classroom down the corridor on the left.'' Her gaze followed me across the room and out of the door.

Jewish prayers! What on earth were they? I wandered down a long dimly-lit corridor, peering in at every classroom window, looking for something which might look like Jewish girls praying. The idea seemed a bit indecent. I had never prayed with just girls before, in fact I had never really prayed. The men always did it on our behalf.

I found the room, struggled with the doorknob, while five faces stared at me in surprise through the glass.

"Turn it the other way," the prefect shouted. She was sitting on top of a desk facing the others.

"Come in, don't be frightened. Let's have a look at you. All right, who do you know and who are you related to?"

"Marilyn, shut up and let her sit down." The prefect smiled and nodded at a chair beneath the desk she was perched on. I sank into it. "Have you brought your prayer book?" she asked kindly.

"No."

"Tomorrow, then."

I made a mental note to ask mother where my ivory bound *siddur*, a bridesmaid's present was.

"We're bound to be cousins. I'm related to everybody," Marilyn whispered over my shoulder.

The other three girls said nothing, and kept their heads down. One of them was twisting her prayer book round and round on the desk.

"Sharon!" She jumped at the prefect's voice. "Your turn to read."

"Er . . . what shall I read?"

"Something from the morning service, of course."

Nervously, Sharon flicked through several pages of Hebrew. "It's very long," she gulped, "where shall I start?"

"Anywhere you like," the prefect snapped with exasperation. "It's all the same."

"Page eight, Sharon," Marilyn chuckled, "the paragraph that thanks God we're neither Gentiles nor women."

Sharon began to read in Hebrew haltingly, faltering over every other word. I sighed with relief. At least when my turn came I could read more fluently than that. The prefect yawned. Marilyn giggled.

"Something funny, Marilyn?" asked the prefect.

"Oh, just passing thoughts," she said, her head on one side, surveying the older girl for a few moments. "Guess who I was with last night?" She rolled her chewing gum under her tongue and held it there. "Danny Greenstone. He took me to Grey's Club."

"I don't believe it, he never takes anyone out."

"He says his cousin likes you."

Marilyn stretched out her legs to one side of the desk. Her black tights were full of holes and the circles of white flesh they revealed were ringed with red nail-polish. I could not imagine why any boy should want to take her to a night-club.

"He hardly knows me. Er, Sharon," the prefect snapped, "keep reading, anything, quickly, here comes the teacher on duty. Let's at least look as if we're praying." Sharon droned on in a dull expressionless voice for a few minutes. We did not dare look up. Heavy footsteps moved slowly past the door.

"Amen," shouted Marilyn, interrupting Sharon's efforts. She slammed her prayer book shut, kissed it, and tossed it on the desk. I caught a momentary expression of hurt on Sharon's face and felt sorry and embarrassed for her.

"Well, his mother told my aunt Phyllis that he'd especially asked at Lisa's wedding who you were."

"Come on girls, the doors are open, time for the notices." The prefect jumped up in a fluster and rushed into the assembly hall.

"Where do we go now?" I asked Sharon, disappointed that the fascinating conversation I had witnessed had come to such an abrupt end.

"Just follow the latecomers and Muslims."

"Do they have Muslim prayers?"

"Of course not. They do their homework."

Then why, I wondered, as we marched into the silent assembly hall and lined up in a row beneath the stony stare of the headmistress and staff, were we made to perform such a charade? I never found out. Was it the same at all church schools? I had my doubts. I only knew it made me

53

feel horribly conspicuous when I would have far rather just been like everyone else.

That was the problem with the "Kosher Dinners", the *kosher* school meals service organised by several ladies at the local synagogue. I had to tramp round the corner on my own in my lunchtime so there was no chance to socialise with my schoolfriends. And then I sat and ate on my own as the other children there were not from my school and I hardly knew them. The food was appalling. Eventually one day we were served fried eggs on lumpy mashed potato—and that for a fortune—and mother relented. I could have school meals.

Despite occasional feelings of isolation I was happy at school on the whole. The creaking floorboards and stone steps were worn down by the relentless tramping of sensible schoolgirl shoes, the long corridor walls were covered with old photographs, children long since mothers and grandmothers. It was like being part of a big, old machine, whose cogs ground on year after year, turning out one generation after the next, the production works of Tyneside's young ladies. We wore bottle-green tunics and Wedgwood-blue blouses, brown socks and mackintoshes tied like sacks in the middle which did nothing for a figure struggling with puppy fat. Hats were compulsory, felt pudding-basins, bought two sizes too large because they shrank in the rain. We tied them under our chins with a tickly piece of black elastic, and whipped them off quickly when we saw the boys from the local grammar school in the distance.

Non-Jewish boys! They were my mother's continual nightmare. What if I should meet one, like one, and—horror to end all horrors—marry one?

"You're of an age now," my mother said to me, when I was fifteen, "when you must understand that you can't go to your schoolfriends' parties."

"But why not?"

"Because they invite . . . boys."

54

"What's wrong with boys?"

"Nothing, as long as they're the right sort for you, the kosher sort."

"But I'm not going to get married yet."

"So don't ask for trouble."

I was rarely able to mix with my schoolfriends outside school anyway. On Saturday afternoons we always went to my grandmother's in Sunderland and in the morning there was the shopping to do. Sometimes I hung around for an hour, waiting for the list. Mother's brain worked strictly in a chronological fashion and it might be eleven o'clock before it reached shopping. Boredom bred resentment.

"I thought we weren't supposed to shop on the Sabbath," I muttered to her, as she chewed the old pencil she always carried round in her overall pocket.

"We're not," she said distractedly.

"But you won't let me play on the hockey team, or be in the school play because rehearsals are on the Sabbath."

"That's different."

Different! How was it different from father doing a Saturday morning surgery, or our going to Sunderland by car? Different because it only spoiled things for me, not them. I sometimes sulked all the way to gran's, staring out of the car window, stubbornly refusing to enter into conversation. We passed small groups of bearded men in long frock coats and shiny black hats, taking a Sabbath afternoon stroll.

"See where fanaticism gets you?" my mother said, turning to me, then jerking her head in their direction. "I can't be like that, but certain standards I must maintain."

"I wish they'd realise this is Britain, not Poland," father muttered, "and it's the twentieth century. No wonder there's still anti-semitism about. I fought for this country you know."

"Haven't I polished your medals often enough?"

55

We drew up at my grandmother's door. Mother turned round and saw the patchwork bag on my knee.

"Shelly, you haven't brought your knitting? On the Sabbath! What will gran say? She'll think I don't know how to bring you up."

I clutched it defiantly and went into the house. Since Mark had gone to London to study sociology I had nothing else to help relieve the monotony.

The noise of the Saturday sports commentary filled the house. Grandpa was slouched in an armchair in front of the television, snoring loudly.

"Wait till the horses come on," gran grumbled, "He'll soon wake up then."

"Had a little flutter again, has he?"

"A flutter you call it? Well you know your father."

"I thought we were forbidden to watch television on the Sabbath," I said self-righteously.

"That's nothing compared with gambling," gran retorted.

"Listen who's talking, with her cigarette hanging out of her mouth," Mother laughed.

Gran shrugged her shoulders and settled down into her armchair. The doorbell went and she nearly jumped through the ceiling. "Quick, quick, where can I put it? I bet that's Moishe and Pearl."

Moishe and Pearl were renowned in our family for their orthodoxy. They even had their house wired so that the lights would come on automatically on the Sabbath. Gran ran over to a plant pot and stuffed the ash and fag end into the soil. Grandpa stirred and groaned. "No wonder I can never grow anything." I kicked my knitting under the chair and sighed. I could not let the family down.

"This Jewish Law," I thought, "I can't work it out. Is it just something adults impose on children to spoil all their fun? Can you grow out of it?" After all, if you were rich enough like Moishe and Pearl, you could get round it anyway. God did not seem to mind the little lapses of most of the Jewish adults I knew. They broke the Sabbath, ate non-kosher food in restaurants, only went to the synagogue when they felt like it—and no thunderbolt from heaven. Even our local Rabbi gave up and told the congregation they could park outside the synagogue instead of in the next street, because everyone knew everyone else had come by car anyway. Did these things really matter to God? Supposing I tried terribly hard to keep as many of the laws as I could remember, I still could not keep them all, and even if I did, I had the strong suspicion it would not help me feel any closer to God. Where was he and who was he anyway that he was worth such an effort?

I went to the synagogue one day to find God. I did not know where else to look. I thought that a religious atmosphere might give that mysterious being, who hid behind the clouds, a chance to communicate. I needed to know more than that he had made me and chosen me. I wanted to know that he was there and interested in me. I wanted to feel his presence. Someone dug me in the ribs, and whispered, "Have you seen John Greenbaum down there? Cor, I don't half fancy him." I turned away.

Behind me, just loud enough for me to hear a large lady said, "Why must Mrs. Davidman wear those ridiculous hats? They do nothing for her." I tried to shut out the chatter and gossip going on all around.

"You, beyond the gilded vaulted ceiling, are you there? Can you hear me?" Silence! The doors of heaven were shut. I felt nothing and went home disappointed.

There were times when life seemed very silly and meaningless. I was sixteen years old, studying frantically, night after night, to get my 'O' levels, so I could do 'A' levels, so I could go to university, get a good job, earn good money, to eat, to work, to eat, to work, to die one day. What if you died never knowing why you had lived? What a miserable existence, what a waste!

Mother thought I was becoming terribly morbid.

"Mum," I said one day, watching her straighten the candlesticks on the sideboard for about the sixth time that day, "what's life all about?"

"Well," she said, moving one candlestick a sixteenth of an inch to the left with the tip of her finger, "you meet a nice Jewish boy, have a nice home, children, cars . . ."

"And then what?"

"When?"

"When you get all that, what then?"

"What more do you want? Oh, you and your questions. Why can't you just accept things as I did!"

Mother's great ambition was to see me married under the *chuppah*, the canopy of flowers erected in the synagogue for every bride. With this end in view, and to provide a little "safe" social life, I was packed off to the Jewish Youth Club, dressed up for the kill. The trouble was, everyone else's daughter was dressed up for the kill too! Still, I bagged my first rabbit in practically no time at all, and took him proudly home.

"What did you say his name was?" mother asked, when the interview was over and the front door safely shut. "It rings a bell. Wait a minute, I know who his father is. Underwear business! No good! You can do better."

I tried again.

"You can't marry him. Something always disappeared at the parties his father went to when I was a girl."

I tried again.

"Family's too orthodox."

And again.

"Mother's only half-Jewish."

When eventually I did drag home a satisfactory conquest called Samuel, a budding solicitor with no conversation, everyone was pleased except me. By that time I had been round most of the boys at the club, and fallen out with most of the girls, so there was little left to go for. There were parties and discos. I spent my life waiting for the next great event, then hating it because it never lived up to my dreams. The real fun was getting ready for them, the long, luxurious bathtime soak, the meticulous work with hairbrush and tongs, the master-stroke with lipstick and mascara wand, the silky feel of new tights. The work of art complete, you make your entry in an expensive haze of perfume and talcum powder. You look furtively round to see who has noticed the great arrival. No one has! Everything is just the same as it always is, same people, same music, same small talk, and you wonder why you bothered.

"There just has to be more than this, but if there is, where is it, and how do I find it?"

My question began to be answered in a most unexpected way. There was a girl in my class at school called Mary. For years I politely ignored her, and when I did not, I was anything but polite. She had long pig-tails, wore National Health spectacles and her skirt flapped around her sensible shoes. Mine had made a temporary halt just above the knees, and that only because school required it. Mary hated pop music and I reckoned myself a real "teeny-bopper". She was the daughter of missionary parents. We were worlds apart. Suddenly I began to notice her. I could not think what it was that attracted me. Perhaps it was something to do with that look of gentle pity in her eyes whenever I teased her or laughed at her. There was no reproach, no sulking, no snappy reply, just a certain quiet dignity, which made her stand out from all the other girls.

"Mary?"

"Mmmmm?"

We were in the cloakroom, struggling into our hockey boots. Her ample form was bent over, bottom towards me. She looked round at me, and straightened up, panting slightly.

"Oh I do hate this awful game."

"Yes, I've noticed. You do tend to run in the opposite

direction when you see the ball coming." She grinned sheepishly. I tucked my knee under my chin. Instinctively she moved over to the wooden bench and sat down beside me. Our heads were half-hidden by the green mackintoshes which hung from the pegs above us.

"The new French teacher, she goes to your church, doesn't she?"

"Yes."

I paused. How could I put into words what I wanted to ask? "She seems . . . a very happy person."

"Yes, she is. Amazing, isn't it, when you think how she nurses an invalid father?"

"Well, what has she got to be happy about?"

"She's a Christian."

"I don't see what difference that makes. You have no choice in the matter. You're either born a Jew, or born a Christian."

"Oh, no, you don't understand. You can't be born a Christian, you have to decide to become one."

I looked at Mary in silence. What she was saying did not make sense. "What is a Christian then?" I asked after a while.

She took a deep breath. "Come to my church and find out."

I shrieked with laughter. The idea of it. Me, go to a church, with my face, for everyone to stare and think I had missed the synagogue? "No thanks," I said, grabbed my hockey stick, and rushed out on to the playing field.

But I could not get Mary's words out of my head. Several of my other schoolfriends began to go to her church and they definitely improved as a result. They seemed happier, kinder, more confident. Was I missing something? What if I went to her church too? Just once, just to see what they got up to, that was all.

5

It was a cold, wet evening, just the night for curling up by the fire in front of the television. I stood at the church gates for ages, looking up at the vast grey building protruding sharply up into an angry sky. The lighted windows beckoned me in, the granite stone walls bid me stay out. "Go away," they seemed to say, "you've no business here."

I took a deep breath, paused to let the hammering in my ribcage subside a little, then let my feet carry me reluctantly across the flagstones, up the time-worn steps, into the gloomy, vaulted interior.

Silence! I can hear myself breathing. There is a vague smell of beeswax, of age and decay. Dead saints glower at me from their gloomy, stained glass windows. Well it's certainly not like the synagogue. No satin and velvet, no crimson and gold. A small pile of books is thrust into my hands. "Oh, thank you." Now what do I do with these? I'll just slip into the nearest pew and pretend I'm not here. No, that would look too conspicuous. The back pews are empty and everyone is down at the front. I keep going, on tiptoes. Heads turn. I am confronted by a sea of staring eyes and curious faces. I wish they would mind their own business. I suppose I must be late, but I really couldn't help it. As usual, mother insisted that I bathe Vicky before I went out, and I could hardly say, "Sorry, mum, not tonight, I'll be late for church." She wouldn't have let me out at all. So I just said, "I have to be at the Club early tonight," and she wasn't really satisfied with that. Well, the Club is only two minutes walk away from here. I'll go there afterwards, and then I won't have told any lies.

Here's an empty pew, right at the end of the row. If I sit here I won't disturb anybody. Arrange your little pile of books in a neat row on the ledge in front of you, like everyone else. Good, that looks impressive. I have the strange sensation of being watched, but when I look up, can't catch anyone actually looking at me. The drone at the front suddenly stops. Long pause, everyone shuffles. Now what? They are all on their feet, chanting something or other. I wish I could find the place. I could pretend I know it or look helpless. Don't know which. Thud! The prayer book has fallen to the floor with a clatter which rings round the building. A hundred pairs of eyes follow my fumbling underneath the pew. I wish my PVC mackintosh would stop making that awful crinkling sound. Why on earth did you wear it today anyway, and the matching hat? You're not exactly a chameleon! I emerge and everyone else has disappeared. They're kneeling. I have never knelt in my life. I'd better have a go. If I don't do the same as everyone else, they might be offended. Which is the quickest way out of this place? Brrr! It's so cold and dreary. I really don't belong here.

The service ended and I was out of my seat and heading for the door when my exit was cut off by a group of friends from school.

"Great you could make it. Coming for coffee?"

"Er, actually I'm just off to a dance at the Jewish Youth Club round the corner."

"Just five minutes."

"Oh go on then, just five minutes."

They led me round to the church hall, a drab, dingy

little building with bare floorboards and peeling paintwork, pushed a thick white china mug of steaming coffee into my hands, and introduced me round. The coffee tasted terrible, but the welcome seemed genuine enough. It surprised me. I mean, why bother to make an outsider feel at home?

They persuaded me to stay for the young people's meeting and I enjoyed it enormously. Someone showed some slides of missionary work in Africa. It was a revelation to me. I knew virtually nothing about anything beyond my own little world. Geography had been abandoned in the third year because it bored me stiff. How could such misery and poverty exist? And how could anyone care so much that they would give up their own comforts, leave the people they loved and go out there to do something about it? It made gyrating at discos and the mindless chatter that went with it seem selfish as well as pointless.

"I could be happy at a youth group like this," I thought. You could talk to people, sit down and discuss all kinds of interesting things.

"Are you coming on the hike on Saturday?" Mary asked, as she escorted me to the door.

"I've never been on a hike before."

"The vicar's a fanatic," she giggled, "so everyone has to go."

"I'd like to, but I'll have to ask my parents."

What would I say, I wondered, as I walked round the corner to the Jewish Youth Club, how could I make them let me go? I pushed open the door, and the blast of pop music drove away any chance to think straight. I hung up my coat in the girls' cloakroom, then joined the row at the mirror with my comb and lipstick.

"Have you seen Marcia in those Lurex trousers? With her bottom! I wouldn't be seen dead in them."

"Ruth looks better tonight than she's looked for ages. That's what I like about her. She tries so hard."

Just like school. The same mindless, bitchy small-talk. My mind was made up!

"Mum, some of the girls at school are going hiking on Saturday. Can I go too?"

"Whose car are you going in?"

"Er, I don't know. One of the fathers', I expect."

"You know how I hate you going out on the Sabbath."

"Oh, let her be, dear," dad said mildly, over the top of the *Reader's Digest*, "it can't do her any harm."

"Can I wear an old pair of trousers?"

"You haven't got an old pair of trousers."

"Well, something that won't spoil if it gets dirty."

"Clothes are not made to get dirty. I don't spend money on clothes for you to ruin them on one stupid hike."

What did it matter. They were going to let me go. That was what counted. My heart thumped with excitement and relief that the inquest was over.

Saturday came, warm and sunny, a marvellous day for an adventure. I was sure mother would find an excuse to keep me at home, and felt sick by the time we set off. Within three quarters of an hour we were in the heart of Northumberland. We abandoned the cars and slung our picnics over our shoulders. I really did not think I would enjoy walking, but was in for a big surprise. I quickly lost track of the time and distance, caught up in the extraordinary beauty of the scenery all around me. At every turn in the path the view was more exquisite than the last. It took my breath away. Why had I never noticed it before? My parents were not great ones for the countryside. "A little breath of fresh air" at the coast was the usual family jaunt, and although I had a passion for the sea and the turbulent drama of its many moods, I had never yet experienced the gracious serenity of the countryside. I stood still, revelling in every new sensation, the wind in my hair, the sun on my back, the gentle bleating of the sheep, the luscious green of the rolling hills and wide open spaces, the exhilaration of being miles from civilisation. Surely there had to be a God who had made all this and given it to human beings to enjoy? Was it really so silly to hope that this God might even want to get in touch with me and help me to understand why he had put me on this earth at all? Looking around me I could not believe that I should have to die one day never knowing anything more about the meaning of my existence than the dreary monotony I had experienced so far.

We found an idyllic spot for a picnic. I could have stayed there forever. We played around on some stepping stones over a brook. I fell in, got wet and dirty, borrowed trousers a size too large and laughed as I never had before. Someone, curled up inside me, who had been sleeping for years, was stirring. It was exciting and frightening all at once. Instinctively I knew that here, just beyond the grasp of my understanding, was the sort of life I had always wanted, but if I pursued it, what then of that other life, the only one I had ever known? That day I had a tiny glimpse of a joy I never knew existed and I could not let it go.

For several months my existence was schizophrenic. I was caught between two worlds. On a Sunday evening I rushed out to the Church Youth Fellowship, and to church too, if an excuse to get out early presented itself. Then I ran round the corner to the Jewish Youth Club, hitched up my skirt several inches and was ready for the disco. Gradually, the world I was supposed to belong to drew me less and less and attendance there became an irritating drudge, a necessity enforced upon me by my guilty conscience about lying. But church services, though still alien and strange, had an increasingly irresistible attraction.

"Have you ever read the New Testament?" Mary asked one day.

"I don't suppose I have," I said, surprised that after several months of slipping surreptitiously into church, the idea had never occurred to me.

"Well, you believe the Old Testament, don't you?"

I nodded. She seemed so certain. Memories of endless translation practice, of Abraham and his desert wanderings. I hardly knew the Old Testament, but I believed in God. Perhaps that was good enough.

"Well, here's a little booklet to help you. Begin with John's Gospel, that's the best place to start."

I took the little booklet of notes out of my handbag that evening and went in search of my old school Bible. It was hidden away in a book cupboard, not exactly dusty, mother would never have stood for that, but certainly unopened for many years. She had been furious when we bought it for Scripture lessons, that we could not find an Old Testament on its own. "We're Jewish," she shouted, in a voice which resounded throughout the shop, "we don't want this end bit." I had tried to disappear under the counter. I could not have cared less at the time, but now I was glad to have the entire Bible in my hands. I tucked it under my arm, ran upstairs, and hid it under the bedclothes.

That night, in the dark, I waited to hear the gentle, even snoring from my sister's bed, then drew it out and flipped through the pages by torchlight. "The Gospel according to John," that must be it. I opened the little booklet. "Pray," it said, "and ask God to help you understand what you're reading."

"O God," I prayed obediently under my breath, watching the shadows flickering across the ceiling, "if you really are there, please let me get to know you, because I don't know how else or where else to find you."

I began to read, slowly at first, struggling with the quaint, archaic language, then faster as the story began to unfold, until, almost despite myself, I was so enthralled that I could not stop, but read on and on into the night.

That was my first encounter with Jesus Christ. I knew virtually nothing about him. Vicky, who attended Hebrew classes at the Reform Synagogue (such was now my father's influence over my mother's weakening orthodoxy), had informed me that Jesus Christ was one of our best prophets; not God, that was a Christian travesty, but a very good man. My father referred to him by some rude Yiddish name. "Jesus, our brother," said one of my cousins. Whatever they thought of him, they actually visualised a cold, lifeless statue with glazed eyes and a pitiful expression. Jesus, the Gentile God, an idol created by the Church to satisfy the imagination of those poor Christians who could not believe anything invisible.

Yet despite everything he always had a secret fascination for me. Years ago mother had taken me to see the film *Ben Hur*, and to her utter astonishment I wept buckets at the sight of Christ, despised and abandoned, bearing his cross to Calvary.

"Jewish girls don't cry at this bit," she hissed loudly.

I gulped and stifled the next sob, but it was no good. Nothing would ever erase from my mind the extraordinary expression of love and compassion I saw in that face.

Although my mother had expressly forbidden New Testament lessons at school, I sometimes lingered at my desk longer than I should, taking an age to gather my books and leave the classroom. Or I stood with one ear to the closed assembly hall doors. I wanted to hear more about Jesus. He did not seem to have done any wrong that Jews should treat him so disparagingly. In fact all I had managed to piece together was the picture of one of the most extraordinary beings who had ever lived. Christians revered and worshipped him. Could they all be misguided? When it came to numbers they had more right on their side than we did. Mother said proudly that that was because we Jews did not proselytise like the Christians. We did not want converts, but I was never convinced that that was the answer.

That night, as I read about him for the first time, Jesus Christ lived for me. This was no remote historical character of two thousand years ago, but someone who was vibrantly alive now, in the present. He became as real to me as the people I sat next to on the bus every day, with the difference that none of them was like this man. He was utterly unique, totally compelling. Every gesture, every word mattered, not just because they made sense out of the mess our world seemed to be, but because they spoke directly to me. That was what was so extraordinary. The more fascinated I became the more I felt our relationship was reciprocal.

"Don't be a fool!" I told myself. "A man who died all those years ago! How can he read your thoughts?" Yet everything he said confirmed the growing feeling that he knew me with a startling intimacy. Nothing seemed hidden from him, no question, frustration or longing, none of the nasty pieces of selfishness that went on in my little head. It was an uncomfortable feeling but I neither wanted to run away nor defend myself with a protective covering of self-righteousness. What was the point? For Jesus, man-kind was obviously an open book. Besides, instinct told me he would not reject me, but rather, unbelievably, that he loved me and had been waiting for me to give him my attention all along.

I was thrilled that when he dealt with the Pharisees he seemed to understand completely how I felt about hypoc-risy. It made him angry too. If I had religion it would have to be genuine, and somehow I could not conceive that this man would offer me anything less.

I read on until one particular statement which Jesus made halted me with a start:

"In my Father's house are many rooms; if it were not so, would I have told you that I go to prepare a place for you?" (John 14:2).

I read it over and over again to make sure I had read it properly. I could hardly believe that here was the answer to the one question which had haunted me for years. No one, not even the rabbis, had ever spoken to me confidently about heaven before. "Do your best," they said, "and then one day, perhaps, who knows . . ." A "maybe" was not good enough for me. If there was nothing beyond the grave, then death made a mockery of every day we lived. Why do your best for something that might not exist? Why live at all?

Was it possible that Christ was right, that there was such a thing as life after death, that he had room in heaven for me too one day? No, it was too good to be true, a fairy story. Who was I to say that generations of Jews had been wrong? What did I know about theology? Still, I could reason it all out as well as anybody else. If there was no heaven or hell, Christ was a liar. How could a man who spoke so much that rang true for me be a liar? He might have been deluded, suffered hallucinations. Then he would have been locked up somewhere for safety. What if Vicky's teacher at the Reform *Cheder* was right, that Christ was a great man, another prophet? But he seemed to suggest he was God. No other Jewish prophet had ever done that before. That was blasphemy. What was left? Only that he was who he said he was, the Messiah, the one my people had been awaiting for so many years.

I shut the Bible, thrust it under my pillow, switched off the torch and tried to get some sleep. My mind was racing. "Take up your cross and follow me." What did it mean? If I followed Christ, would I have to say goodbye to my family, friends, and traditions, the only life I had ever known? They would certainly say goodbye to me. Oh no, God, no, not that, I can't.

Get a grip on yourself, stop being so silly, who are you talking to anyway? A God who lives way beyond the galaxy in untouchable splendour. As if he cares about a tiny dot like you!

The next night I got my Bible out and began to read

again. Philip, the disciple, seemed to put my dilemma into words:

"Lord show us the Father, and we shall be satisfied" (John 14:8).

That was it, what did God look like? I had never dared formulate a mental picture of God before. There are never any paintings of him in Jewish books or synagogues. That would be a transgression of the commandment never to make a graven image. Somehow that had transferred itself to painting pictures in my imagination too. Christ's reply took me aback:

"Have I been with you so long, and yet you do not know me, Philip? He who has seen me has seen the Father" (John 14: 9).

I understood. The very things which attracted me to Christ reflected the personality of God, his Father. At last I could give my imagination the freedom it longed for. I could begin to see God.

I never realised how disconcerting that kind of an exercise could be. My conscience had never particularly bothered me before, but now I felt as if a pair of unseen eyes was watching everything I did. The long hours spent snogging at parties filled me with distaste. Words and deeds over which I would never have thought twice began to affect my peace of mind.

"Dodging the busfare, that's stealing!"

"Telling lies again?"

"That was a hurtful, catty remark!"

I felt that God was sitting in heaven, judging everything I did, and everything I did was such a miserable failure. Could he ever forgive me? Would I ever be any different?

Some six months after that first tentative venture into a church building, a school trip to York was arranged to see the Mystery Plays. A weekend away with friends was a rare treat and as the coach set off from Newcastle my pulse raced with anticipation. By evening the rain had benevo-

lently acknowledged our pleadings and petered out to a
light drizzle. Waterproofed to the hilt as only the English
know how, we trundled in a straggly crocodile into the
floodlit castle grounds, then found our places amidst dozens of other school parties. Someone handed out the tof-
fees and chewing contentedly we huddled closer together
to keep out the chilly evening air. I had not realised that
the Mystery Plays were medieval interpretations of biblical
stories from creation to the end of time, but somehow
seeing the Bible portrayed like that as a whole made me
realise just how much the New Testament was a continua-
tion and completion of the Old.

As darkness fell and the lights on the immense stage
beneath us were turned up, the munching and wriggling
slowly stopped and the performance took on a magical
quality. The crowds around me ceased to exist. The hard
wooden bench which moments earlier had seemed to bite
into my backside no longer vied for my attention. I was
entranced, aware only that as we moved inexorably on to
the crucifixion we were reaching the climax of the evening. Christ was on trial, was booed, hissed and rejected.
A vast cross was dragged across the stage and the Roman
soldiers stripped him and nailed him down with blows
which resounded right across the York Castle grounds. As
the cross was hoisted into the air with Christ stretched out
upon it, suddenly everything fell into place for me, and I
understood what I had been reading for the last few weeks.
I wanted to leap up and down and shout, "That's it! I've
got it! That's why Christ had to die, for me, for my sins,
so that I can be forgiven and have eternal life," but I held
on tight to the bench instead.

I was dizzy with excitement. All the self-reproach, the
sense of failure and emptiness which had weighed me
down for years and made me feel unable to look God in
the face was offloaded onto that cross and hung there with

Christ. This was the real freedom he spoke about. Blow the cost, I would follow him whatever it meant.

The performance ended. People got up, laughed and chattered. I sat very still. I did not want to move. I wanted to hold on to every minute for as long as possible, to try and make some sense of it all. Someone dug me playfully in the ribs with the end of an umbrella. In a daze I followed the other girls back to the guest house, almost unable to speak for the strange gurgling sensation in the pit of my stomach. I wondered whether to stop one of them, Mary perhaps, but what would I say? "Something very important has happened to me tonight." It sounded a bit forced, even a bit corny, so I said nothing and sauntered along in my own little world, blithely oblivious of everything around me. Besides, I had neither the comprehension nor the vocabulary to explain whatever it was that had happened to me that evening, although I knew I should never be the same again.

6

"Mary?"

"Yes?"

We had been heading for the ice cream van in the ten-minute interval of the Mystery Plays. Mary had been gingerly stepping on the grassy-looking bits of the field to avoid getting mud all over her shoes and tights, but without much success. She looked up at me distractedly. Her glasses had slipped to the end of her nose.

"What's the Holy Spirit?"

"Who, you mean."

"O.K., who?"

"Well," she took a deep breath, then sighed heavily, "you do ask difficult questions at such funny times. I'll tell you later, when we get back to the guest house."

She kept her word, and later that evening, when the six of us who shared the rather dowdy guest house bedroom were in our pyjamas and tucked up in bed, she padded over to me in her furry slippers. She picked up my Bible, opened it at the beginning of the Book of Acts and said, "Read that. If there's anything you don't understand, ask me tomorrow."

I wanted to tell her what had happened to me, but did not know where to begin. I opened my mouth, but she was half-way into bed. I read for a while, and when I next looked over at her, there was a loud snoring sound coming from her open mouth.

"I still don't understand about the Holy Spirit," I said the next day, after a rather restless night.

Mary sat down on her bed. It sagged several inches. "It's like this," she said, "the Holy Spirit is part of the Trinity." Trinity! It was an alien word. I shuddered slightly. "I mean, he's the third part of God. He comes to live inside us, when we're Christians, to help us live a Christian life."

"So that's all right for Christians," I murmured, "but what about me? I don't know what I am any more. I suppose I'm nothing now. I don't belong anywhere."

The room went very silent. The four girls who were sprawled on their beds, recovering from a service in York Minster and Sunday lunch, looked up incredulously. Joanna, the Head Girl, put down her book. She always spoke with great authority. "Oh, but you are something! You are a Christian."

A Christian! How could I be a Christian? I was a Jew. What made her say that? Was it because I now attended a Bible study group she and Mary had started at school? I had never realised before that you could actually discuss the Bible and learn something from the mistakes of men like King David. Or was it that driven by an inexhaustible curiosity to know about God, I had started to creep like a criminal into morning assemblies, feeling conspicuous and uncomfortable as if I were betraying a sacred trust and everyone knew it? I had always sensed that Joanna sympathised with the agonies of conscience I had had to overcome in order to do it.

But Jews did not become Christians! The very word was a contradiction of all that being Jewish meant. I felt confused and my face must have registered my struggle for comprehension. Everyone watched me for a while. No one spoke. I allowed my mind to wander back to the previous evening and relived that extraordinary moment when both Old and New Testament had come together and I had gazed on a tapestry woven with great harmony and precision, instead of a tangled mass of skeins. The crucifixion made sense of everything. Christ had received the punishment I deserved so that I could be forgiven. God's forgiveness was the missing piece in the jigsaw puzzle which I had been searching for all along. That was what Judaism had been unable to promise me.

"Yes," I said slowly to Joanna, breaking into the silence, "you're right, I am a Christian." Their faces suddenly stretched into the most enormous beams. I watched her and Mary and waited. "I'm a Christian," I repeated a little more confidently. It still seemed a very strange thing to be saying. "Oh horrors!" I gasped as the full realisation of what I had just said finally dawned. "What will my parents say?"

"Don't be in too much of a rush to tell them," Mary said wisely. "Let them see the change in you and they will ask the questions." She was right, of course, I was a different person. They would be stunned by the startling transformation. I would be loving, helpful, patient. After all, the Holy Spirit lived in me now. He would do it all!

For a few weeks I floated through the house on air. Sheer joy made washing the dishes and making the beds quite bearable. But gradually the ever-increasing list of tasks which mother's fanaticism for tidiness imposed on the household stirred up such a mass of frustration that I could not swallow it any longer. I exploded with rage. I managed not to throw anything, and thought that must be a sign of progress, but I still felt awful. I said so many things I never meant to say, and I was a Christian! I had ruined everything.

I was still in a state of dejection as Christmas approached. My first Christmas as a Christian. What a failure I had turned out to be! God could not possibly still love me. On Christmas morning I was at my post, by the bedroom window, wash leather in hand. Mother insisted that every window in the house be wiped down with three different cloths, three times a day. She had a horror of condensation. That tiniest patch could so easily turn into a drop of water, that drop became a trickle, the trickle a flood and the flood would damage the curtains and ruin the carpets!

I stood still and stared out at the people slowly making their way to the church at the top of our street. The intense longing to rush out and join them welled up inside into a terrible ache. I made myself continue wiping, my fingers so frozen that I could hardly feel the cloth. Suddenly I became aware of an invisible presence standing right next to me, so close that I was afraid to reach out a hand, or breathe, or move at all, lest it vanish. I was overwhelmed with the sense of comfort and joy. It was as if Christ himself had opened his arms and drawn me into them, holding me tight, just as my father had done when we were younger. Somewhere inside me a voice seemed to whisper, "I am Emmanuel, God with you, God very close to you. This is the only Christmas present you need." I held on to the moment as long as I could, dreading being left alone again. Yet long after the wonder of it had died away, I knew that Christ was still beside me. He understood what I was going through, and knew I was not always to blame for the outbursts I could not control. He would share the boredom, the loneliness, the frustration and the tears. I would tell him exactly what I felt, and he would help me to cope. He was right. To know that he was close by was all I needed.

Day after day I wrestled with the growing inner conviction that I would have to tell my parents what had happened. My stomach turned over and I felt slightly nauseated at the very thought. They would never understand. It would seem a betrayal, the worst thing I could possibly do. I could not hurt them like that. The stigma in the Jewish community alone would be terrible. I could almost hear the gossip and see my parents slinking away in shame.

"Their daughter . . ."

"Did you hear?"

"Isn't it tragic?"

"Who would have ever thought?"

In my bed at night countless agonising scenes would act themselves out in my mind in glaring technicolour and I would bury my head in my pillow desperately trying to shut them out.

"Christ is with me, Christ will help me," I repeated to myself over and over again, but I had no idea how. "Oh let them see the new me," I prayed. "Let them make some comment about it, and then I shall say, 'It's Christ who's done that, he makes the difference,' and they might just be the tiniest bit glad."

But the day never came. It was no good wriggling out of what I had to do. We were close enough as a family for me to hate the deceit and lies. Finding excuses to get out early on a Sunday night was becoming an impossible strain. Besides, I sometimes felt that my parents knew what I was up to. A bit like the proverbial ostrich, they stuck their heads in the sand. Suspicion was easier to live with than truth. Only a year to go until I left home to go to university. I would wait until then. It seemed by far the most sensible idea. If things turned out for the worst, at least I would have a bolt-hole.

I hung on to the prospect of university like the survivor of a shipwreck to the piece of timber he hoped would carry him to the distant shore. Studying French was a small attraction compared to my deep need for freedom and independence. "Durham," I wrote as my first choice on the university application form.

"Durham?" my French teacher queried. She had taken to spending a few moments alone with me whenever possible, sometimes to explain a Bible passage I had been reading and did not understand, at other times to listen to my tales of woe and advise me if she could. "Durham's only twenty minutes away by car. Shouldn't you be exploring further afield?"

How could I explain the panic I felt at the thought of leaving everything and everyone I loved? It vied constantly with my longing to escape and be myself, two entirely conflicting emotions in a desperate struggle for supremacy. In Durham I thought I had found a compromise.

"Where else would you like to go?"

"Well, I'd like to do drama as well as French and that's only possible at Hull, Manchester . . ."

"Manchester? Put Manchester down as your second choice."

"Oh, I don't really want to go there."

"Yes, but it has a good French Department by reputation, and . . . I don't know why, it just has a certain 'feel' about it."

I did as I was told, it could do no harm. Durham was bound to accept me. A letter came from Manchester with the offer of a place. They demanded high 'A' level grades, but it was a place. I waited. Then one morning there on the mat lay a long white envelope with "University of Durham" written in black letters along the top. My fingers felt like lumps of plasticine and the few seconds it took to tear the envelope apart seemed interminable. The letter was simple, but as I read it, I felt stunned, as if someone had landed their fist sharply across my jaw.

"We regret we are unable to offer you a place . . ."

Disbelief gradually gave way to anger and I flounced into school that morning in a fury. Mary emerged from the sixth form cloakroom and peered over the banisters to see whose arrival was making the wooden staircase creak more than usual.

"Oh oh," she said and disappeared back into the cloak-room. I followed her, flung my mack over a hook, and rammed my outdoor shoes into a cubbyhole. She watched me in silence, a rather bemused expression on her face. It was by no means the first of my rages she had witnessed. I went to the mirror and attacked my hair with a comb.

"Durham," I said, between bared teeth, "have rejected me."

"That doesn't surprise me."

She was behind me and I could see her face in the mirror. She was smiling. I refused to comment.

"Look," she said impatiently, "did you or did you not give your life to Christ? Don't you think he has the right to say 'no' sometimes?"

"But I want to go to Durham," I shouted, threw down my comb and marched into the classroom, with the sound of Mary's gentle laughter behind me.

She was right of course, but I did not discover that until later; there could be no possible compromise between my need for security and the search for self-discovery. The former would have swallowed up the latter and destroyed any chance I might have had of maturity as a Christian, let alone as a person. I had to go further from home. Looking back with the wisdom of hindsight I was thankful that God did sometimes say 'no', not just to thwart me and spoil my fun, but because he understood the intricacies of my emotions better than I did myself. The objective nature of his love for me enabled him to make by far the most sensible decisions for my future. And so I packed my ample belongings into an enormous trunk and set off for Manchester University.

I spent my first day trailing around identical high-rise faculty buildings, searching in dozens of dark corridors for obscure room numbers, sitting in endless queues, filling in piles of administrative paper, thus proving I was intelligent enough to become a fully-fledged undergraduate. Then we "freshers" were let loose on the Union building and told to present ourselves to the societies of our choice. The surging mob carried me up the steps and pressed on ahead while I lingered to read a sign which said, "Entry Forbidden to Those under the Age of Eighteen." I was seventeen and not used to ignoring instructions. I gingerly stepped inside and was immediately catapulted into a world which was louder, more garish and belligerent than any I had ever seen before. Every available inch of wall was plastered with cheap posters, bearing weird names and even weirder drawings. The corridors were lined with makeshift stalls made out of trestle tables, each representing a different society, each manned by students determined to lure in the innocent and the unsuspecting. I was bombarded with hand-outs and deafened by the hullabaloo.

The floor, littered with discarded advertising, almost felt like a carpet beneath my feet. I wandered around in a daze feeling lost and very alone. Where should I start? The French Society or the Drama Society? But there appeared to be dozens of drama societies and I didn't know which to choose. Then I remembered that when we had said good-bye Mary had warned me it would be like this.

"Make sure you look for the Christian Union," she had instructed me in a maternal sort of way. I had nodded obediently. "I don't want you falling by the way. And anyway, they'll have your name. I've sent it to them already."

"She's certainly taking no chances," I thought.

Standing in the middle of the Union building I felt more like running away than falling away. "Excuse me," I whispered to a young man in faded, frayed blue jeans who was leaning idly against a wall, but the blast of pop music drowned me completely and he went on tapping his foot to the insistent drum-beat, totally oblivious of my presence. "Excuse me," I tried a bit louder, "could you tell me the way to the Christian Union stall?"

He suddenly realised there was something at the height of his elbow which was not going to go away and looked down. "Eh?"

"The Christian Union," I shouted. The sound of my own voice startled me and I shrunk another inch.

"Down there," he sneered, jerked his head, then turned away. "In with all the other religious nuts."

Religious nuts! His contempt took me aback. As a Jew I had come to live with disdain, as a Christian it was totally unexpected.

I followed the general direction of the jerk of the head and eventually came out into a quieter, sunny room. It was full of stalls: Methodist Society, Baptist Society, Catholic Society, The Anglican Fellowship. It suddenly struck me how strange and sad it was that Christians divided themselves up into these silly little groupings. A Jew was a Jew however he chose to worship, but there were countless brands of Christians.

My reflection was disrupted by the sound of laughter from the other side of the room. A group of people were chattering with great animation around one particular stall. I looked at the wall above it and read "Manchester Inter-Faculty Christian Union" in huge red letters. They stopped their conversation and looked at me quizzically as I approached, then broke into smiles of greeting when they realised I really had found the stall I was looking for.

"Hallo, where are you from?"

"What's your name?"

"Which hall are you in?"

"What are you studying?"

"Just fill in this card, will you?"

81

Someone handed me a pen. I obediently filled in the card, then the pen was taken from one hand, the card from the other. The latter was studied with great interest by a girl with enormous brown eyes and an infectious grin. "I'm Hilary. I see you're in Langdale Hall. Ruth is the rep there. She'll look after you."

"Rep?"

"Yes. She's responsible for organising the Christian group in your hall. She'll tell you all about Bible studies, prayer meetings and the like. Now, here's a Christian Union programme too. We've some fantastic speakers coming this term. Are you coming on the hike on Saturday by the way? Oh good, you'll soon get to know lots of people."

I could have hugged her with relief, but felt a little too overwhelmed at that precise moment. As I turned away I suddenly noticed the neighbouring stall for the first time. The large blue Star of David on the white cloth draped over the trestle table was unmistakable. I did not need to look up and read "Jewish Society" on the wall. A dark-haired girl manning the stall caught my gaze and stared at me with marked curiosity. I averted my face, but knew I was still being watched.

"She knows I'm Jewish," I thought. "I could have picked *her* out as a Jew anywhere."

I was tempted to go and speak to her, drawn by a sense of belonging and mutual understanding, but instead I turned round and walked away, feeling a strange mixture of guilt and embarrassment. Her eyes burned into my back. Why could I not join them? I had every right to do so. Blind panic told me that if they knew that I was a Christian they would not accept me. I would end up in another horrible maze of lying and deceit. And anyway, I had been seen at the Christian Union stall. The truth could not be concealed for long. Whether my fears were well-founded or not I could not risk the possibility of having to justify myself or

82

their rejection, not then. Too many changes were taking place both within and outside me. Too bad if it seemed like running away. There was so much to get used to. I needed time.

That first year in Manchester was a great adventure. Life was so hectic that after the first week I had little time to feel homesick. I loved the city itself, the glittering metropolis with its elegant buildings, theatres and concerts, which for a Geordie lass had all the glamour of London. And I had the freedom to succumb to its many attractions. The University was just near enough to the city centre to pop in for an hour's shopping between lectures or a curried salad lunch at the Ceylon Centre.

I did not manage much work, just stared helplessly at endless booklists and wondered where to begin, but the social life was better than anything I had ever imagined. For the first time I met Christian boys! The church youth group back in Newcastle was virtually all female. Any specimen of the male variety of the species who actually came to church never dared to brave such a gathering for two weeks in succession, but the Christian Union was full of them. There were the handsome, the charming, the shy, the awkward, the considerate and the masterful, an endless variety from which to choose. My head spun.

And then there was the rapture of being able to attend any Christian meeting I wanted, without shame and fear of being found out, without planning explanations all the way home. The term became a whirl of Bible studies, prayer meetings, planning meetings, coffee parties, houseparties, parties of all kinds. I was not going to miss anything. Like a sponge I soaked up every drop of Christian teaching available, all the more so as the prospect of the first vacation loomed nearer and nearer.

My parents were proud and thrilled to have a daughter at university. Manchester too, where we had those nice relatives with the eligible son! They missed me, and were greatly looking forward to the vacation. I walked back into the house for the first time after several months with a sinking feeling in my stomach. I looked round at all the familiar objects, all in their usual places, pill bottles in neat little rows, cups upside-down on saucers, ready for the next drink, cold coffee in an old metal coffeepot, ready to be reheated for the next morning's breakfast. The dog rushed out to greet me, wagging his tail furiously. I bent down and stroked his head. He stayed very still and I wondered if he sensed my mood. This was it! Better get it over with as soon as possible, but what on earth was I going to tell them? How could I bring such disruption to their world and destroy all the high hopes they had placed in me?

Over supper I was bombarded with questions. How were aunty and uncle? And what was their son like, the one who was studying medicine? Did I like university? Was I settled? I answered their questions briefly, reassured them I was enjoying Manchester very much and went on eating my meal. Mother looked slightly troubled, shrugged it off and began to clear away the dishes.

"Mum, dad," I said quietly. My hand was shaking and I tried to control it. "I've something to tell you." Mother put the dishes down and dropped back on to her chair. She would not look up at me. My father wiped his mouth on his table-napkin and put it on the table. "I've . . . I've become a Christian."

No one spoke. I looked at them, and could hardly bear the pained expressions on their faces. I tried to say, "But this doesn't really change anything, I'm still Jewish, I'm still your daughter, I still love you," just as I had rehearsed it dozens of times, over and over again in my mind, but the words refused to come.

"You've been going to church, haven't you?" my mother demanded.

"Yes."

"That it should ever come to this, a daughter of mine going into a church."

"Now don't get into a state, dear, it's these friends of hers. They've influenced her. She'll grow out of it, won't you?"

I shook my head.

Father looked suddenly bewildered. "Where did we go wrong? How have we failed you?"

Mother broke down and wept violently. "No *chuppah*! Never to see my daughter married under a canopy. I'll be the laughing-stock of the entire community." So that was what really mattered, what the relatives thought. Anger broke through the hurt I felt at what I was doing, and gave me the resolve to stand firm and weather the immediate crisis.

It was the first of many during that vacation. My mother spent most days wandering miserably around the house, muttering, "What are we going to do?" "She'll survive," I thought. My father worried me more. He was unnaturally quiet and thoughtful, and I often caught him looking at me with great tenderness and pain in his eyes.

"We can't go on like this," he murmured, after yet another scene, with everyone pleading and weeping their way through the box of tissues. "We're not getting anywhere, so let's be sensible about the whole thing. 'Honour thy father and thy mother' is one of the Ten Commandments, isn't it?" I nodded, blowing my nose and drying my eyes. "Well, I can't help but feel you'd give up this 'Christian' business if you really believed that. Still, I think you'll grow out of all this. You're not twenty-one yet, so we still have some say. While we can't demand it, we want you to promise not to be baptised, or to go to church."

"Or take that bread and wine they eat," mother inter-

85

rupted, "and we'd like you to see a rabbi, I've rung him already, who'll teach you more about Judaism, and answer some of your impossible questions. Oh, and we want you to stop reading your Bible, and please," tears flowed again copiously, "don't go out with any non-Jewish boys."

I weighed up their words carefully. They had a right to see that I still loved them and wanted to honour their wishes. "I agree to everything," I said, swallowing the lump in my throat, "except that I must read my Bible."

"You'll read as much Old Testament as you read New?"

I nodded. They sighed with relief, and gave me a hug.

"Well," said father, "let's get on with life, shall we?"

There was a letter waiting for me when I got back to my hall of residence in Manchester. Rabbi Gold would like to have a little talk with me, at my parents' request. I explained everything that had happened to the small Christian group who met in hall to pray and study the Bible together. It was such a relief to share it all.

"Pray for me, girls," I said, "because God only knows how I'm going to survive the next three years without going to church or going out with boys. And what on earth shall I say to this rabbi?"

My tummy felt tight and I was breathless when I tapped at the Rabbi's door. A secretary ushered me into the waiting area outside his study. I sat chewing the skin round my nails, reminding myself over and over again of the Bible verses my friends had given me!

"And when they bring you before the synagogues and the rulers and the authorities, do not be anxious how or what you are to answer or what you are to say: for the Holy Spirit will teach you in that very hour what you ought to say" (Luke 12:11–12).

He emerged moments later, not as I imagined a rabbi, a tall, gaunt, clean-shaven man, with a prominent nose and small, penetrating eyes. He had his arm around a younger, rather good-looking man, and as he showed him out he called after him, "Don't forget, let me know how you get on."

A nod seemed to suggest that I follow him, and another that I take a chair. I perched on the edge, bracing myself for the first assault.

"So why have your parents sent you to me?"

He knew why, surely. I was not playing "cat and mouse". "I've become a Christian."

"How does a Jew become a Christian?" he asked slowly, with a hint of mocking irony in his voice.

I told him my experience as briefly as I could. Was it my imagination, or did he seem slightly shaken?

"The boy," he said, "the one you saw, who was in here before you, he said exactly the same things." He paused a while, and stared unseeingly out of the window. I prayed he was reckoning me a hopeless case and would let me go. "Well, well, what do you want to ask me?" The tone became dismissive.

I tried to think up some suitable questions. "Isaiah, chapter fifty-three?"

"The Suffering Servant, yes?"

"Well it says that the Messiah would be 'wounded for our transgressions, and bruised for our iniquities'. That describes Jesus Christ on the cross. It's obviously Jesus Christ. He fulfilled the prophecy. That makes him the Messiah."

The Rabbi smiled and shook his head. "I think not. The Suffering Servant is Israel, the nation."

"How can Israel be 'a man of sorrows and acquainted with grief'?" I asked, genuinely puzzled.

"In the Scriptures Israel is often referred to as a person."

"Oh." I was not satisfied, but had no means to argue. "God answers my prayers now."

"And mine too."

"I don't know what to say. All I know is that before I

was utterly miserable, but now I have something which makes life seem worthwhile.''

''And you know what this is doing to your parents? It will be the death of your grandparents.''

I nodded and got up. I had to get out.

''Before you go, I have a friend, a Church of England minister, who will help you appreciate what it means to be a Jew. Will you see him?''

I shook my head. I could not stand any more. I ran out into Albert Square and walked round and round, until I felt calm enough to get on a bus. Though I did not know it, I had just turned down a premature opportunity to meet my future father-in-law.

One clergyman I did see was the minister of the church I attended in my first term. He had been contacted by the Vicar in Newcastle and invited me round for a little chat. Once again I found myself sitting in a clerical study walled with books from floor to ceiling, feeling slightly intimidated. But this man was fatherly and kind.

''I hear you've promised your parents that you won't go to church until you're twenty one?''

''Yes, I want them to see that I'm bending over backwards to honour them.''

''But you can't go on like that, not for more than a month or two.''

''But I must, I've promised.'' I was beginning to feel the hot prickly sensation at the back of my neck I was coming to associate with pressure, however gentle.

''You need fellowship, the support of others, Christian teaching.''

''But I get it all in the Christian Union without breaking my word.''

Smiling he got up and showed me to the door. ''I'll give you a month,'' he said, ''then see you back in church.''

As the door closed behind me I made up my mind to be guided only by an inner voice. If I listened to everyone

88

else I would end up torn in a hundred pieces and strewn across Manchester from church to synagogue.

For most of my time at university I managed to keep my parents' wishes. I was quite relieved to have an excuse for not going to church. I still did not feel at ease in that environment, and found that the multiplicity of meetings laid on by the Christian Union more than made up for what I missed. In fact, as I grew more confident about being a Christian, I realised that Christian meetings could swallow up every bit of available spare time, that one's horizons could become very narrow and restricted, and so I ventured out into the secular world, joined a drama society, acted in plays at the University theatre, got involved in student local radio and became captain of the hall table-tennis team. There was hardly time to breathe and I tried to push home to the back of my mind. It made the vacations harder than ever.

"Yes, Samuel, she is free tonight. I'm sure she'd love to go out with you." I hung over the banisters, shaking my head furiously, as mother put the receiver down. "Such a nice boy," she said smugly, "he seems so keen on you. Do go out with him. It'll be good for you, take you out of yourself a bit." I gave in. I felt so helpless. Poor Samuel. If he only knew how he was being used. Then suddenly I had an idea.

"Samuel," I said that evening, as we drove up to the house in the dark after a lavish meal, "there is something I have to tell you. I'm not what I seem."

"Oh?" He wriggled uncomfortably.

"I think Jesus is the Messiah. I mean, I'm a Christian, so you won't want to see me any more."

"Are you going into a convent?"

"No, but it means a lot to me. My life is so different now. We're miles apart."

"You can believe what you like. It doesn't bother me."

"O.K. Well, see you around. Thanks for a lovely evening."

I rushed into the house and breathed a sigh of relief. He never rang again. Mother was puzzled.

"You know," she said one day, "I'm sure it's because you never gave him a goodnight kiss. I watched you from the window. Boys like a little bit of that."

We jogged along in an uneasy truce for a number of years. Mother watched me anxiously, desperately hoping for a sign that the crisis was over, then giving way to utter wretchedness when she saw that the Bible was still on my bedside table. I said nothing, and kept the Christian side of my life very much to myself. In Manchester I joined a group of students who met to worship together on a Sunday morning. They attended house churches when they were at home and did not like institutional church services. I identified with that, and enjoyed the informality and spontaneity. We were regarded as something of a dissident group by the rest of the Christian Union.

"Don't go there," I was warned. "They're very extreme. They speak in tongues."

I was on my guard and did find the garbled, muttering sound which went on as people prayed under their breath very strange at first. Their ecstatic expressions and raised hands made me feel uncomfortable too, but what drew me was that they seemed to love God in a way I did not. I appreciated him for the things he gave me, forgiveness and the peace inside that went with it, eternal life and the promise of a place in heaven, but loving him for himself alone, that was something different altogether. I read a chapter from the Bible every day, but it no longer thrilled me like it did at first. Praying, too, had become very routine. "Are you filled with the Holy Spirit?" they asked me. "Well, I received the Holy Spirit when I became a

90

Christian, didn't I?" "Yes, but there's much more than that. You need to be baptised in the Spirit, filled full to overflowing." What did they mean? Whatever it was, if there was a dimension I had missed, I meant to have it. "I haven't fought all this way to get only half the goods," I thought. "Fill me with your Holy Spirit, Lord," I asked, "because I do want to love you like they do."

He answered when I least expected. No noisy, emotional, "whizz-bang" experience! But one day, when I bumped into Hilary on the Union steps and quite spontaneously we had decided to find a quiet little room upstairs to spend some time praying together, in the stillness I became aware of God's presence in a way I had only once experienced before, that Christmas Day years ago, when I had been drying the windows. Only this time the sense of God's nearness did not fade. It became increasingly real. His love seemed to flow in waves all around me and I relaxed and allowed myself to be carried along in the ocean.

"So this is what heaven is really like," I thought, "this utter rest and peace, this endless warmth and comfort and enjoyment of God's presence!" I did not want to return to reality, fearful that the moment would evaporate into nothingness, but it did not. The new awareness of God's love and greatness stayed with me, transforming my routine Bible study and prayer life into the language of a love affair, making all I thought I had sacrificed seem paltry and insignificant. Worship came easily, I wanted to spend time with God.

"You couldn't call that Sunday meeting 'church'," I told myself. "You are still keeping your part of the bargain." Or was I? The niggling at the back of my mind refused to go away. I was twenty-one. Had the time come to re-open the old wounds?

I moved to a flat in Didsbury and began to attend the local Free Church there. The agreement with my parents was a thing of the past. I realised with a heavy heart that we would have to talk again. Besides, the church had a baptistry. I watched several of my friends being baptised and knew it was only a matter of time before I would have to follow. I kept putting it off. I told myself it was an unnecessary extra, that it was unreasonable to hurt my parents again. One day, as I was reading through the book of Acts, a verse almost rose off the page, as if it were illuminated: "And now why do you wait? Rise and be baptised" (Acts 22: 16). I could not go on running away from that inner voice. "All right, Lord, you win," I shouted, "but I can't tell my parents, not now, with my final exams on the horizon."

"You know what baptism means, don't you?" The minister looked down at me with an air of gravity and compassion. "It's a public demonstration that you belong to Christ."

"I know." I hung my head. He put his hand into his pocket.

"Here's the key to the vestry. Help yourself to the telephone."

I wandered across the half-empty church in a daze. Unfortunately the key slid into the vestry door lock without the slightest effort. The room smelled musty. I sat down weakly beside the phone, lifted the receiver, and waited a while for my heart to stop pounding. My fingers trembled on the dial, then somehow found the right numbers. It was ringing. Oh, let them be out, please!

"Hello! Oh, it's you darling, how are things?"

'Mum. I'm going to be baptised." The silence seemed interminable. "I said . . ."

"I know what you said.'' The voice was cold and hard. "Never come home again. You're no longer our daughter." Click! The line was dead. I put the receiver down slowly. When the minister appeared at the door a few moments later, I looked up and saw to my horror mascara-stained pools of tears splodged all over his crisp white writing paper.

I was baptised on Whit Sunday with little elation and a great deal of pain. "I'm doing this because you ask it," I whispered to God, "not because I want to, so don't expect me to enjoy it." Everyone around me seemed thrilled. They fussed me, hugged me, petted me, but I felt numb. Afterwards, I went back to my little flat and sat alone in the dark. "O God," I whispered, "why didn't you make me a Gentile? It would have been so easy then."

7

I would sometimes study my face in the mirror, sigh and think how nice it would have been to see a blonde, Scandinavian-type goddess staring back. But there she was, that rather swarthy looking character with the dark, unruly curls, the olive complexion, that nose infuriatingly large compared to other small features. I tried fluttering my eyelashes and pouted for effect. She pouted back and looked, I thought, passably sultry and continental. But I was sick of being asked if I were foreign. I never knew what to say.

"No, actually, I'm English," never seemed to convince anybody, except once in a crowded restaurant. A studious looking gentleman at the next table peered at me through the spectacles on the end of his nose. When he had finished his meal he leant across and said, "My dear, permit me to say what fine Celtic colouring you have."

The friend I was with giggled into her table napkin. "No Celt, here, mate," she whispered to me.

"Semitic actually," I said to the gentleman, smiled sweetly and went on eating my chocolate mousse.

"What I want to know is," I confided in the mirror, "when people pass me in the street can they tell that I'm Jewish?"

"Does it really matter?" the reflection enquired.

94

"Of course it does. Let's be honest. If people say 'Jew' at the first glance, their preconceptions will affect how they see me before I open my mouth."

I never forgot an experience which happened when I had only been a Christian for a matter of weeks. I was with a group from school, on our way to a Bible study at the local boys' grammar school, when a boy passing us in the corridor stopped, pointed a finger and jeered, "Look at that Yid." The corridor, one moment raucous with end-of-schoolday noise, suddenly seemed very quiet. My clothes stuck to my body. I felt awkward, conspicuous, too humiliated and stunned for anger, as if I had been slapped across the face. I could not respond. To my annoyance no words would come. Then there was a peal of laughter and he and his friends disappeared. My friends pretended not to notice and continued our chit-chat.

Becoming a Christian so radically shook my sense of identity that it became imperative for me to discover what being a Jew really meant to me. It never mattered before. It was a fact of life, something to be embraced alternately with joy and resignation.

"You're still a Jew of course, aren't you?" my Christian friends said to me, but which part of me was "still a Jew"? How could I be so sure? It was illogical, irrational, but reason did not enter into it. I knew I was a Jew because I still felt Jewish inside. It was an entirely emotional response, yet here, unwillingly, I had discovered why even the least-practising Jew will adhere belligerently to his radical, if not religious, identity. What matters is what I feel, not what I do.

If there was one phrase I heard more than any other as a child it was, "I'm not a good Jew, but I am a proud Jew." It was said with such gusto, such assurance, that I thought being a proud Jew must earn you such a vast tick on your credit column that when the Almighty balanced the books it wiped out all the debits of deliberate law-breaking. One day I suddenly understood. There are times when people repeat a phrase over and over again with great certainty and dogmatism in a desperate bid to convince themselves of its truth. Jews are not always fearless of what others might think of them. Deep down inside, perhaps at a subconscious level, many must have felt as I did that day in the boys grammar school, small and very worthless. The real terror is not that others might abuse us, but that they might be justified in their abuse. Debase and despise a people for long enough and they will almost be convinced they deserve it. That was the hangdog attitude which drove six million Jews into Hitler's gas chambers with barely a murmur or a protest. We were helpless, defeated.

No Jew can come to terms with being Jewish without coming to terms with the holocaust. I could look at it objectively as a historic event, be appalled at the degradation of human behaviour, even grieve for the relatives I never met, but that was not enough. Amongst Jews genetic bonds are very strong. Each Jew seems to carry in his bones the tragedy and sufferings of his entire race. It was not enough to wonder what it would have been like if I had been there, then bury the feelings in the depths of my subconscious when they became unbearable. One thing was certain, if I had been born twenty, even ten years earlier, in Germany, Poland, Holland, Czechoslovakia or France, I would have been transported to a concentration camp. In that it happened to my people it happened to me, and I had to allow myself to experience the absolute hell of it. Nightmare followed nightmare for several months, as my emotions wrestled to resolve their inner turmoil. I felt the terror of that uncertainty in the overcrowded cattle-trucks, the ache and pain of bereavement, the humiliation of becoming a faceless, nameless piece of human flesh, the stench of hatred and loathing exuding from the bodies of our persecutors. Then the dreams stopped. I had reached a total acceptance of what it meant to be Jewish, the conscious awareness that time and time again throughout history one has had less value than horse manure.

How one uses that knowledge is crucial. It has produced the dedicated Zionist, convinced that a homeland is the only solution, the aggressive Israeli who has discovered that for the first time a Jew can actually fight and win, the materialistic entrepreneur, seeking security and acceptance in wealth, and the extraordinary cultural and intellectual achievement of the Jewish people in recent years born of centuries of brokenness and rejection. I too had a choice to make. I could allow my Jewishness to have a negative influence, read anti-semitism into the most meaningless word and gesture, or I could use it positively, learning to trust and forgive. Ironically, it was my experience of the Church which drove me to the crisis point and forced me to a definite decision.

For three years I had honoured my parents' wishes and did not attend a church, but nor had I mixed in a Jewish environment either. I temporarily postponed making any real decision about who I was or where I belonged. I clung tenaciously to my experience as a Christian and my identity as a Jew without emotionally being able to bring the two into any kind of inner harmony. I had not grown up. As I became more involved in the rather conventional Free Church where I had been baptised the realisation suddenly dawned upon me that while Christians patted me on the back and whispered soothingly, "Of course, you're still Jewish," it meant nothing at all. In fact, although it was never actually said, I began to feel that most people hoped I would settle down and become a Gentile as quickly as possible. I could hardly blame them. After all, the early Church was not sure how to cope with the problem of converted Gentiles and the Jewish Christians wanted them to become Jewish as quickly as possible too.

It was a great temptation to blend like a chameleon into

97

my new environment, to be safe, secure, wanted, to pretend that I had never known any other life. I could wipe out the pain of my parents' rejection, hack off my Jewish past, throw it into the deepest recesses of my subconscious and begin again, a totally different person. It would never work. The process would have involved a radical amputation, leaving me scarred and mutilated, not whole at all. Besides, pretence is a dreadful strain to live with. The past would have haunted me like a restless ghost, making unwelcome appearances at the most inconvenient moments. That was not the abundant life Jesus had offered me. He was a Jew himself, he had accepted me as a Jew, surely Christians could as well. Was it really fair of people to criticise me for being "too emotional", "too independent", "too outspoken", "too noticeable", "too unconventional"? I was sick of being taken into a corner and being told that for my own good, I really ought to know that certain church members had expressed concern that . . . !

The problem was that this was my first real encounter with the institutional Church, albeit in its Free Church disguise, and we did not get on too well. Occasional church attendance had been one thing, commitment was another altogether. I suddenly realised that a "take it or leave it" attitude was no longer possible. Somehow when I took Christ and made him mine I also managed to acquire the institutional Church, a bit like Jacob with his Rachel and his Leah, and I definitely had not expected that part of the bargain.

"Free Church services will be much freer than the Anglican services you remember," I told myself, "much more spontaneous and informal." But there it was, week in, week out: hymn, prayer, hymn, reading, hymn, sermon, hymn; a triple-decker sandwich with the minimum weekly variation in the filling. The sermon was always excellent, but how I wished it did not seem that in order to get there we had to dispense with the rest as quickly as possible. I thought worship was supposed to be important. Was this it, this standing, singing, sitting, slouching, in strict obedience to the voice at the front, this dull, dry ritual enacted by a hundred marionettes devoid of every indication of human emotion? It left me cold, unmoved, unable to participate. Even a smile could freeze on your face. Religion is a serious business! I thought it false and hypocritical to hide behind a mask of piety during services.

The Victorian decor did not help matters. Coloured glass windows set in mullion stone, coated on the outside with the grime of years of Manchester traffic, shut out the daylight. The low timbered ceiling, though pine, had been painted with the dark brown varnish so fashionable at the turn of the century. In my flights of fantasy I would climb up there with a tin of paint-stripper and a brush. How many months would it take to restore it to its original golden beauty? But it would be worth it. The wood-panelled walls were caked with dark brown varnish too. The loose wooden blocks in the parquet floor clattered and squeaked when someone shuffled on their chair. I sometimes felt I was enclosed in an airless, dark brown wooden crate and had to fight the urge to get up and run outside into the sunshine.

Where was the noise, the colour, the emotional vibrancy of the synagogue? I had never realised how much a part of me they were, the haunting quality of the Hebraic chant, the easy natural alternation between prayer, song and chatter, the dazzling shimmer of the scrolls as they were carefully removed from the crimson-curtained ark, then lovingly carried round so that the men and children could kiss their prayer shawls, then reach out and touch them. In the intensity of my search for God I had been so full of Judaism's inadequacies that I had forgotten its sheer joy and beauty, until I was deprived of it. In the middle of church services memories would flood over me in a huge, irresistible wave, filling me with a sudden, terrible panic.

"What am I doing here? How did I get here? I don't belong. Let me out, please."

And then I would remember I had nowhere else to go. The festivals with their gaiety and laughter, the family traditions I loved so much, had gone forever. At my baptism I thought I had found a new family, but it did not quite work out as I expected. Sunday after Sunday I walked home from church alone and sought refuge in my little flat; interminable Sundays, full of hurt and loneliness.

"It wouldn't be like this in the Jewish community," I moaned. "Someone would have invited me home on the Sabbath."

The more I grieved for the world I had lost, the more I sunk into a morass of self-pity and anger, with the Church as the primary object of my resentment. Christians could not do anything right. Like a porcupine, I was all wound up inside and covered with protective prickles on the outside.

"In Ephesians," says the preacher from the pulpit, "in chapter two verse twelve, Paul tells the Gentiles that they were alienated from the commonwealth of Israel. That speaks to each one of us today."

I squirm on my chair. "Speak for yourself."

"When the Jews crucified Christ . . ." the preacher continues.

That makes me really mad, but there is worse to come.

"Now that God has finished with the Jews, we Christians are the chosen people, the new Israel."

Finished with the Jews! Well, why am I sitting here? Why have we been so persecuted? If God doesn't still love us, who does? Just wait until the service is over. I'll tell him a thing or two, and anyone else who happens to be in range.

To the credit of my Christian friends, they endured my

100

tempers, tantrums and explosions, as I wrestled for my identity, with more grace than I deserved. If only they knew how much I hated my own behaviour. I did not understand it. I could not seem to control it. I wanted to bite my stupid tongue off. Patience was supposed to be a fruit of the Holy Spirit. If only it would plop, like a windfall, into my lap. I would do better next time! And then someone had to discuss Middle Eastern politics with me. So kind of you to take the time to explain the Arab point of view. I'm sure they have one, but do you really expect me to see it? My people have never had a land to call their own before. We don't belong anywhere. No one ever wants us. Inside me a voice was crying, "And do you, a Gentile, really want me, a Jew, in your Church?"

There seemed no outlet for my Jewishness at all, and it was an immense frustration, particularly as I was constantly discovering how Jewish Christianity was.

"Look," I said excitedly at a home group one day, as we were exploring the meaning of Jesus' words, " 'For where two or three are gathered in my name, there am I in the midst of them' (Matt. 18:20) Don't you see? In Judaism no act of public worship is valid without a *minyan*, a quota of ten men. Jesus is saying, 'Forget it, two is all you need for my presence to be with you.' "

"Oh yes, very nice," everyone said, and smiled at me indulgently.

Certainly New Testament passages were real for me in a way I could see they were not for others. I could never hear the verse, "For he [Jesus] is our peace, who has made us both [Jew and Gentile] one, and has broken down the dividing wall of hostility" (Eph.2:14) without wanting to leap off my chair in a paroxysm of joy. But my smiles only met blank stares. I could have shaken the congregation one by one and shouted, "Don't you see what Christ has done? Here we are together, though normally we'd have nothing in common, and years of mistrust would

101

have held us miles apart.'' But they did not see it, and sadly I wondered whether in taking my being a Jew for granted, they did not take the extraordinary reconciliatory work of Christ on the cross for granted too.

What was I to do? I could not continue like this, writhing on my chair in the agony of believing I could preach better sermons than those I was hearing. I sat down one night in the quiet of my little flat and weighed up all the possibilities. I had tried to conform, to be what everyone seemed to expect from me, but that had not been the answer. I could not sustain the performance for more than a week. Or I could fritter away my life lamenting my lost past, just like the children of Israel in the wilderness, looking wistfully back over their shoulders, idealising the Egypt they had left behind:

''. . . the leeks, the onions, and the garlic'' (Num. 11:5).

''Let's face it,'' I thought, ''if Judaism was that wonderful, why was I converted in the first place?'' Just like the children of Israel my persistent moaning was blinding me to the many good things in my new inheritance.

The only remaining possibility was to learn to live with myself, explore the riches my Jewish background had given to me and seek, somehow, to share them with the Church. That sounded good, but how could it be done?

''Oh God,'' I pleaded in desperation one night, ''here I am, feeling such a mess inside. I want a Christianity which really works, so please sort me out, will you, and while you're at it, do something useful with my life.'' Slowly, very slowly, he answered.

Several months after my baptism I rang home for the first time.

''Er, mum? It's me. I've got my degree.''

''Oh yes?''

''Will you come to the graduation?''

''We'll see. We'll let you know.'' Click! The phone

102

went dead. They said they might come, there was a glimmer of hope. I hung on to it and was rewarded. There, among the last cars to swing into the carpark, was the familiar shiny white Volvo.

My heart pounded as I went to meet them. It was a hot day. I felt wet and sticky beneath the weight of my gown. Mother checked me over from head to toe with a glance, straightened my hood, then frowned when she noticed my tangled, limp curls. We walked in silence to the graduation ceremony, then afterwards stood together on the steps of the Arts building and smiled for the official photographer.

"Where's your luggage?" she demanded, when the ceremony was over. I could hardly believe my ears. "Get the car," she barked at my father. "It's time to go home."

"I presume you went through with it?" mother asked in a very controlled voice, after we had journeyed in heavy silence for some half an hour. She did not even turn her head.

"Yes," I whispered from the back of the car.

I saw her reach out and pat my father's knee with her hand. "We might have been so proud of you today, and instead, this. You come home as a stranger, you realise, not our daughter."

That first evening I was sitting alone. The house seemed very silent. Father appeared at the sitting-room door, wearing his skullcap. "Have you a moment?" he asked.

"Of course."

I followed him up to his bedroom, and saw his prayer book lying open on the bed. He picked it up uncertainly.

"I've been trying to pray," he said, the words choking him slightly. "Funny, isn't it, me, an agnostic, wanting to pray? I need someone to pray with and don't know who else to ask. Will you pray with me?"

He took up the prayer book, and we read together, in English. I slipped my arm through his and saw that there were tears in his eyes.

"You're a great comfort to me, you know," he said.

Gradually my parents and I rebuilt our shattered relationship, but not as it was before. To my amazement it was much less fragile, stronger, more stable, based on their acceptance of my adult decision to live my own life. No more blind dates, no more playing their 'Fiddler on the Roof' record in the hope of creating some sudden, emotional return to the fold on my part. They let go, and as they did I discovered a freedom to love them I had never known before. I loved them for accepting me despite everything their consciences told them, I loved them for making no further demands despite their own pain.

I felt a great need to be alone with God, to walk, to think, to understand this unexpected gift he was giving me. As I did so memories came flooding back, many adolescent and childhood scenes which had caused great hurt, words which had left unhealed scars, just waiting to open and ooze again. The feelings of rejection I associated with becoming a Christian had much deeper roots than that. They were buried in my subconscious. I felt as if God were opening a hundred tiny doors to the corridors of my mind, which I had kept tightly shut for years, and inviting me to go with him on a guided tour of inspection. A small group of close friends sat with me and prayed as a whole series of incidents from childhood and beyond, of which I could have no conscious recollection, enacted themselves before me. The hurt was almost unbearable, but the healing God seemed to pour into those gaping wounds made the temporary discomfort infinitely worth it. Anger, resentment, pain were carried away by copious tears.

"My daughter, let me have that chip on your shoulder, that feeling of utter rejection. Do you want to know where it comes from?"

"Where, Lord? Show me."

I heard an inner voice as if I were a little girl:

"The *Goyim* don't cook like we do, the *Goyim* don't

live like we do. Never trust a *Goy*. They despise us. And even if you marry one he'll call you 'dirty Jew' in the end.''

"But I don't really believe that, do I Lord?"

Rationally, of course, I did not, but something of that attitude remained deeply embedded within me like a cankering sore, inhibiting my ability to feel at ease in the Church, and form open, trusting relationships there.

One Sunday morning, during a time of open worship in the morning service, an exciting and refreshing innovation for the church, I falteringly asked for forgiveness for all the bitterness I had felt. If it had not been for Gentile Christians I would never have found Christ at all. If it had not been for their love and perseverance my survival as a Christian might have been in jeopardy. I am not sure the apology was understood, but it was graciously accepted.

I was determined from now on to use my Jewishness positively and enrich the Church in whatever small way I could. If there are hundreds of years of pain and rejection locked in the heart of every Jew, there are also hundreds of years of worship buried there just waiting to be released when the Messiah comes with the key. I had not discovered a new religion or a strange new God, but the God who had always been there, with my ancestors down through the centuries, with me in the rituals of my childhood, only I had not recognised or known him. If I was Jewish through and through so was the Church, from its founder and foundations to the book that inspired it. One day it would wake up and begin to explore the Hebraic cultural roots it had ignored for so long. I wanted it to happen overnight, that was my mistake. But happen it would and I was going to do everything in my power to help it: introduce feasts, festivals, celebrations, all the treasures of the Jewish heritage. Besides, the wind of change was now in the air. Charismatic Renewal began to affect the whole Church and not just a few individuals on

105

the fringe. Old preconceptions were shaken, some conventional attitudes overturned. There was a new interest in Hebraic music and dance. The time was ripe for innovation.

I now began to find the confidence and freedom I needed to make a point of going home for the major religious festivals. Besides, Judaism had begun to make sense in a new way. The ritual of eating bread and drinking wine on the Sabbath Eve was a small foretaste of the Communion service. Kindling the *Chanukah* lights at the Feast of the Dedication of the Temple was a visual reminder that Christ was the light of the world, come to give light to all men. But it was the Passover which thrilled me most of all. It was the same old service I had loved as a child. But now, as we read and sang together, I imagined Christ eating his last meal with his disciples, his own heart heavy because he knew what was coming. Yet he used the rich symbolism as an audio-visual aid, so that they would understand why he had to die, that he was the real Passover lamb, the Afikomen, broken for the sins of the world. He took:

"In the same way also the cup, after supper, saying, 'This cup is the new covenant in my blood' " (1 Cor. 11:25). The cup taken after the meal was the third cup, known as the cup of blessing. Christ's blood was shed so that death would forever pass his children by. I gazed at Elijah's goblet with gratitude. In every Jewish home it would always stand untouched. The Messiah had already come.

Two places at our Passover table were conspicuously empty and gran wept her way through the entire service. The new joy I found in the traditional words and symbols was checked by her terrible pain and our loss as a family. Grandpa died after a stroke had left him paralysed and speechless for two years. When his only son, Mark, was born, so totally unexpectedly, seventeen years after my mother, grandpa had exclaimed with enormous satisfaction, "Now I have my *Kaddish*." Only a son can recite those special prayers for the dead and keep alive his father's memory by having his name and taking his place in the synagogue. Mark came home for the funeral from Peru, where he was a journalist. For seven evenings, the duration of official mourning called "*Shivah*" after the Hebrew word for seven, his glorious voice resounded round the house as he sang those ancient words, "*Yis gadal va'yis kadosh sh'may raboh . . .*" (*Glorified and sanctified by God's great name . . .*)

Six months later he was dead, too, after a tragic accident. He was twenty-seven and had no son to say *Kaddish* for him. His coffin was flown home for burial in the Jewish cemetery in Sunderland. Only my father could bear to lift the lid and look for the last time at the sleeping face, wrapped in the prayer shawl he had so often worn in the synagogue. For the second time in six months the rabbi took a pair of scissors and made long cuts in the clothing which mother and gran were wearing, an old tradition dating back to the time when people rent their garments in grief and despair.

"Why?" gran shouted at the ceiling, "Why, why? There isn't a God! There can't be a God!"

The women sat together trying to comfort her, as David led the men in the all too familiar prayers in the next room. They mourned a life cut short, wasted potential, the children Mark would never father. As the sound of their lament drifted through into our room mother turned to me, looked at me inquisitively for a while, then said, "If only I had your faith."

"You can," I whispered, desperate to bring her some kind of hope. But she just shook her head sadly and looked away.

Prayers ended and one by one the visitors filed past the bereaved to pay their respects.

"What's this I hear about you then?"

To my embarrassment I realised that Geoffrey, one of my mother's cousins was addressing me.

"You've become a Jehovah's Witness or something? I know Mark defended you to the hilt. He was adamant you should be allowed to follow your own conscience." To my surprise Geoffrey's smile conveyed genuine interest, not paternalistic indulgence.

"I've become a Christian actually."

"Really? Tell me about it won't you? I'd love to chat."

This was a conversation I had never anticipated. I had become so used to a negative response that it took me some time to lower my defences.

Being a Christian in a Jewish environment and a Jew in the Church began to be extremely enjoyable. When it came to the latter I discovered there could be great advantages in coming into the Church without any denominational bias, without any knowledge of long-standing Christian traditions. One could have a very objective approach to what was valid and biblical, and what were extraneous cultural additions.

"It must be marvellous to be free from the law," gushed a well-meaning middle-aged lady after she had heard me speak about my conversion. I was always being asked to "give my testimony" in church after church ad nauseam, until I felt a bit like a combination of a freak specimen and a prize poodle.

"Oh yes," I said, anxious not to quash her enthusiasm, but embarrassed by my own hypocrisy.

"Free from the law," what did it mean? Jewish laws had not really been an encumbrance to me. It was impossible to remember all of them, let alone do them. If Jews really believed that keeping the law earned them God's favour they would be much more careful. In observing those we chose to observe and ignoring the rest, the law had served us. How could I explain that in the few seconds of a snatched conversation? "Yes, thank you, I do enjoy

108

an occasional pork chop now." We had always gone out to restaurants for our pork chops anyway! How could I make her see that in fact some Christians had a system of laws more terrible and tyrannical than anything I had ever known as a Jew, a veritable evangelical Torah?

"Thou shalt not smile in church."

"Thou shalt not wear make-up."

"Thou shalt not go to the theatre, the cinema, dances, nor anything which could be classed as worldly."

The whole lot could be summed up in one glorious commandment: "Thou shalt conform."

Sometimes the Church felt like a vast machine which swallowed up its members, ground them to powder, then pumped them out again, model Christians, numbered and coded without any personal identity or individuality. I fought the process with all I had. Why give in to a puritan, Victorian anachronism?

One incident which happened while I was still at university made me smile whenever I thought about it. It was a Sunday evening and I was unpacking my suitcase in my little box of a University hall of residence bedroom after a weekend at home. I was in a turmoil of a hundred different emotions and very tired. Mother had bought me a lovely new dress, bright red and cut away at the shoulders. I could not resist wearing it for the journey back to Manchester. There was a timid little tap at my door.

"Come in."

It opened slowly, and Ruth, who was in charge of the hall Christian Union group, peered round it. "Can I come in?" she murmured, staring at the floor.

"Of course you can. Why the formality all of a sudden?"

She did not answer, or look up, but shuffled sheepishly into the room. Those ridiculous old slippers!

"Seat?" I nodded at a spare bit of bed next to my suitcase. She perched on the very end and examined her fingernails.

"Shell?"

"Mmmm?"

"I, er, Sylvia told me to come. She thought, and I did as well, that I ought to talk to you about, er, the way you dress."

Sylvia was vice-president of the University Christian Union. She was wise, she was spiritual, she gave up her fiancé because he was not a Christian. She spoke and we obeyed. I felt hot and sticky all of a sudden. "What bothers you in particular?"

"Well, your hemline for a start. It's barely decent. Christian men have a hard time keeping their thoughts pure. With you around it's twice as difficult."

I looked down at my knees. They were nothing marvellous. I wondered whether to feel flattered.

"And just look at that dress." Ruth was warming to her subject. "Look where the stitching goes. Talk about suggestive."

For the first time I noticed two rows of white topstitching making two circles on the front of my dress.

"Ooh, yes. Is that bad? Will it upset somebody, do you think?"

"Sylvia and I, we think that you should succeed me in leading the hall group, but really, it does depend on your behaving more as a Christian girl should." She got up and began to back to the door. In a funny way I respected her for saying what she felt she had to. She had not found it easy.

"O.K. Ruth," I said, too weary and stunned to say anything else, "I'll try."

"Oh, and by the way," she delivered her parting shot from the safety of the doorway, "even your nightie's red and frilly."

"Well, drat," I thought, "she's even been peeping under my pillow."

I flopped down on the bed and sat there thinking for

some time. I had to admit it was a bit daring, not to mention a bit chilly, almost to reveal my underwear. My legs were too short anyway. It was just that some of the girls in the Christian Union were a bit old-fashioned, even dowdy, and I did like to shock. But then I never had a boyfriend like some of my Christian friends. So many Christian men seemed dreadfully mild and timid. I had a sneaking suspicion that they were frightened of me. I was either too foreign, or too fast, and looking down at my hemline and the circular stitching on the bodice of my dress, it was not hard to guess which. I should have to reform a little, I decided, for the sake of happy, open relationships, not because someone had held out the carrot of position and responsibility. Hang ambition! It was not exactly Christ-like, hardly a virtue worth the cost of conforming. I would be true to Christ and what I understood to be his will and true to myself.

God had used his creative skills to make me with all my foibles and idiosyncrasies, a Jew who was a Christian as well. I could look him straight in the eye exactly as I was. Let the minister's wife say, "If God had intended you to have green eyelids you would have been born with them." If God had not intended her to have a shiny nose why was she not born with it ready-powdered?

I lost a great deal of excess weight and for the first time in my life felt very glad to be me. There was just one problem. I had a degree, but no job, and no certainty of what I wanted to do either. One thing alone was clear.

"Oh God," I said one evening, watching various huddled shapes pass beneath my flat windows in the twilight drizzle, "let me never forget what I've felt like these last few years, and let me bring the joy and wholeness you have given me to those who feel as lonely and insecure as I did once."

8

I never meant to fall in love. It was an added emotional complication I could have well done without, especially in my final year at university. But there he was, that tall, rather composed sort of character, with the gentle voice and brown velvet eyes, smiling at me across the room in a Christian Union meeting. My stomach turned cartwheels. Suddenly all my noble aspirations to serve God in whatever way he wanted were overtaken by a host of uninvited daydreams, of romance on desert islands, white wedding veils, and terry nappies hanging on the washing line.

Then came the devastating blow. It was painfully obvious that my affections were not reciprocated. I could not believe it. How could God let this happen to me? Had I not given up enough for him: home, family, community? How dared he refuse me the man I wanted too? I yelled and raged at the Almighty, wept and stamped my foot. It was not fair. It was all his fault. I never wanted to feel like this.

"It's so easy for you," I told him, "you can make Peter fall in love with me in a second, or make me stop. So why don't you?" I suppose I thought he was some kind of celestial Eros, who, having misdirected a fiery dart, would say, "Sorry dear, my mistake," and either pull mine out or shoot one at Peter too. There was no response from the heavens. What was the use of telling God that he would never again find anyone as suitable as me, that Peter's family have been interested in the Jews for generations, that we had so much in common? He would neither be bull-dozed nor blackmailed into giving me what I wanted. I would somehow have to trust that he did know what was best, even if it was beyond my comprehension, even though Peter moved into a flat barely a quarter of a mile away from mine and started to attend the same church. At least I could still have his friendship, his presence at various social occasions, his figure to stare at surreptitiously from behind my hymn book every Sunday morning. But that was all I had for a very long time.

Since there was evidently no immediate prospect of marriage on the horizon I still had to discover what I was meant to do with my life. I might have to watch Peter walk down the aisle with someone else one day. I might never marry. The idea filled me with horror, but all around me were single Christian women in their thirties and forties. Why should God not ask it of me? Although it was not easy, better face it and accept it than spend years mooning around waiting for Mister Right. After all, there were some positive advantages in having no ties and few responsibilities.

"Have your fling dear," my father said with a knowing wink.

"Fling?" my mother expostulated. "Who needs a fling? At her age I was a mother."

She had taken to making loud comments about "young, glamorous grannies", and "the blessing a grandchild must be", whenever I was within earshot on social occasions. To my parents' despair the only "children" I acquired were anything but desirable. I became a youth worker.

Working with delinquents and drug addicts had seemed romantic to some of my friends, but never to me. I had intended being a teacher, but felt very unsure about it. In

113

my final year at university I applied to do a certificate in education, mainly because everyone else did, and set up a record in the French department of being rejected by all six colleges of my choice. If I was not meant to teach, what was I meant to do? I staved off any decision by working for a Master's degree, and never got it. Fascinating though Wagner's influence on French literature might be, I was soon fed up with musty libraries and nothing but books for company.

I only called at the Manchester Youth Services out of vague curiosity. Helping at a Youth Club occasionally might bring me the fulfillment which research did not.

"What experience have you of working with young people?"

"Summer camps."

"None at all. I see."

"I once stopped a girl committing suicide on me."

"Fascinating. How about doing the real thing, say helping at a youth club for one or two evenings a week, to see if you like it?"

"Fine."

I felt my face coming under intense scrutiny, and I knew what was coming. "At a Jewish Youth Club?"

"Great!"

"There's one just round the corner from where you live and the youth worker happens to be the best in the Manchester area, in my opinion. He'll train you well, if youth work's what you want to do."

That evening I walked round to the synagogue and stood for a while outside the huge wrought-iron gates. From my flat window I had watched the congregation come and go, and wanted to join them, but had never dared. Well, here I was after all. The gates creaked open with a little pressure, and I followed the stream of light and blast of pop music into a large hall full of teenagers who immediately stopped what they were doing to stare at the stranger who had just slipped in. I looked around at the many faces, some swarthy and very Jewish, others fair and light-eyed. Some were open and animated, full of expectation, others were hostile, bored already, suspicious of anything new. Eight years vanished in a moment. I was transported back in time to my own adolescence with all its anxieties and insecurities. I might have been back at the youth club in Newcastle. It was a decidedly uncanny feeling.

"Come into my office, darlin'." The high-pitched voice with its strong Cockney accent startled me back into the present. So this was Ernest Bates, the youth worker. "D'yer smoke?"

"Me? No."

"Good, ruins the natural body odours. What do yer do?"

"Er, a bit of drama."

The tiny eyes, which never left my face, reminded me of two black beads stuck into a round wooden ball on which someone had painted lips and cheeks. Everything about the little middle-aged man, from his shorn haircut and baggy tweed suit to the briefcase, which dwarfed him, was conventional to the point of old-fashioned. A more obvious Gentile in a room full of Jews would have been hard to find.

"I'm a *Goy*, yer know."

"Yes," I muttered, convinced he was reading my thoughts.

"But I don't stand for any nonsense. If any non-Jewish youngsters come in here, they keep their hands off the opposite sex. No marrying out. It's more than my job's worth."

"There's something I'd better tell you then."

"Oh yes?"

"I am a Jew, but I'm a Christian too. I became one a few years ago."

"Oh gawd, not one of them. I've met your sort before.

115

Trust my luck to get landed with one. Yer not going to convert us all, are yer?'' He laughed so raucously I thought he would be heard above the music in the next room.

"If I'm asked about it, I can't lie."

"All right darlin', you do yer own thing, only don't cause me any trouble."

Ernest Bates lived up to his reputation for training youth workers. Once I had got used to his rather strange sense of humour I was grateful for his astute and honest assessment of my progress, or the lack of it. With all expenses paid for by the Association of Jewish Youth, I joined a training course he had organised for several volunteer workers.

"Where did you say you were based?" the other students asked, disparagingly. "A Jewish Youth Club? You can't call that the real thing, can you? I mean, those kids are hardly socially deprived. They're middle-class, they've got money, too much of it. A good spanking would be more use to them than your help." I thought of Simon, struggling to cope with eighty per cent deafness; Jackie, a spastic neglected by her parents, desperate to prove she was as intelligent as anyone else; Julie, an adopted child, bewildered and confused, not looking at all Jewish, but raised in an extremely orthodox home, and the others, all with their own particular anxieties, trying to come to terms with belonging to a minority culture, most of them living with enormous pressures: to achieve, to marry well, to please parents and community. How could anyone be stupid enough to suggest that their needs were less than anyone else's, that they would be spared the trauma of growing up?

I was just beginning to be trusted at the club, to feel I was of some use, when the crisis occurred. A journalist from one of the local Jewish newspapers popped into the club to see what went on. "What exactly do you do?" he asked me.

116

"Well, I seem to sit in the Ladies' most of the time. The girls like to chat while they put their lipsticks on."

"Youth Worker Spends Her Evenings in Ladies' Loo," went the headline. The kids spread the newspaper out on the bar and shrieked with laughter when they read it.

The editor of the rival Jewish newspaper was not so amused. He had heard me speak on Radio Manchester about being a Christian, noted the name, and when he saw the article, knew he had a scoop. This time I was given a front page spread: "Christian Youth Worker Proselytises Our Youth." I could not believe it, it was so untrue. I dashed to the telephone.

"So it's you, is it?"

"Oh, Ernest, I'm so sorry."

"How could yer do it? How could yer give the man an interview?"

"He tricked me. He said he wanted to talk to me about youth work."

"I could have told you what he was like. Don't suppose you've read the editorial?"

I had. It began, "How long must we employ a Gentile youth worker . . .?"

"It's me they want rid of," Ernest bellowed. "Ah, well, I've weathered worse storms than this. But do me a favour, don't show yer face round here again." When next I heard of Ernest he had a lecturer's post in youth work at a polytechnic.

I wished I had been able to say goodbye to the kids, to offer some kind of explanation, rather than slink off like a criminal. A few days later the phone rang. "Michele? It's Julie. Hope you don't mind my ringing. Can I meet you in town? I'd like to talk to you."

We sat in the Kardomah Cafe two days later. Julie giggled into her kona coffee.

"If Dad knew I was meeting you he'd kill me."

"I can imagine." Dad was quite a bigwig on the Synagogue and Youth Club committees. He must have loved me! I studied Julie for a while. She was striking already, with her long blonde curls and vivid blue eyes. She created havoc among the boys, who found her English-rose attractions quite irresistible. The girl who seemed to have everything, but behind that bounce and sparkle was someone who felt very lost and very unloved. Suddenly she became grave, struggling for the right words.

"That article in the newspaper," she said, then looked straight at me, and for the first time I saw the hurt, and the tinge of anger in her face. "Was it true? I mean, did you really only help us to get us converted?"

"What do you think, Julie?"

"I don't know. I'm so confused. Everyone says you did and they feel betrayed. They're furious, but I don't ever remember you trying. That night, when I was so upset and you sat with me, I thought, here's someone who's really interested in me, but now I don't know any more."

"Julie, I do care. I've become very fond of all of you."

"Then why? What made you convert anyway?"

"Well, I suppose, just like the article said, I was looking for something I didn't find in Judaism. I was fed up with religious hypocrisy, and like you, I was fed up with the superficial social routine, and I felt that something was missing, that I wanted to know who God was. I read the New Testament, and though it's hard to explain, when I read about Jesus Christ he seemed the most real, the most honest person I'd ever come across. The things he said made Judaism make sense at last. Realising he was the Messiah was the missing link."

"You amaze me. You're quite nice looking. You could marry a nice Jewish boy, settle down, have a pleasant, easy life, but instead you chose this."

"Funny, isn't it? Sometimes it amazes me too, but I wouldn't change things. When you find something that answers all your questions about why you exist at all, it's worth any price you might pay. And I suppose, had any of you asked me about it, I would have told you. I can't actually convert anyone. I can tell you what happened to me, but then it's up to you. You have a mind of your own.''

''I think I understand a little.'' Julie was smiling now. ''Can I see you again?''

''I'd like that a lot.''

Julie was the first of several youngsters from the club to seek me out and demand some kind of explanation. The editor of the Jewish newspaper achieved more than he dreamed of! I was thrilled, but it still did not alter the fact that my research grant had run out, I was unemployed and had to find money for food and rent. I scoured the newspapers for a job, but nothing seemed right. ''Something will turn up,'' I said. Was it faith or fatalism? I think it must have been the former, because my confidence was quickly rewarded. A couple of days after I had given up looking, the telephone rang.

''Hello, my name's Frank White.'' The voice on the other end of the receiver was warm and friendly, and its soft, Geordie lilt aroused my instant affection. ''I've just come to Manchester to work for the Catacombs Trust, a Christian detached youth work project. It's grant-aided by the local authorities, who are represented on the committee by Ernest Bates. I told him I wanted a colleague and he tells me you're just the girl I'm looking for.''

It sounded like a proposal.

Although we knew before we met that there were too many coincidences involved already for me not to be the right co-worker for Frank, he still needed to see flesh and blood to be finally convinced. I chose my wardrobe carefully, not too trendy, but not too conventional either, and felt a total anachronism as I walked into the Manchester City Mission. No mortal had been at pains to redesign its mournful interior since Queen Victoria ended her glorious

119

reign. The chapel was tiled in green and white like a public lavatory, hushed voices floated eerily out of several tiny offices, two old tramps huddled up with misery, sat in a corridor, waiting to be attended to. I wondered if Dickens had been here once and found inspiration.

"I'm up here." Frank was leaning over a rickety wooden staircase. "Come up. This attic's the office."

As he looked down at me I saw curiosity give way to a quickly suppressed smile of approval. A face which gave everything away, that was a good sign!

The office was tiny, barely big enough for one desk, a filing cabinet and two people. "How do you bring kids in here?" I asked.

"You don't," he grinned. "One look at this place and they'll be off. They'll think it's haunted."

I sat down on the one chair and Frank perched on the end of his desk. "Well, all I have to do now is persuade the committee I need you."

"And do you?"

"Oh yes, a man out alone at night on the streets of Manchester! I can't approach a girl, and I'm just discovering I can't approach a boy either."

His look of comic indignation made me laugh. I liked him enormously straight away. He was relaxed and easy. With his tattered khaki hat pulled half over his eyes, he reminded me of a stray mongrel, and that touch of the vagabond added to his charm.

"Yes, you do have a problem," I admitted, "and I'd love to help you solve it."

The committee was convinced. How much pay did I want? I hadn't a clue. I thought of a minimal figure and they seemed quite satisfied. No one knew where it would come from, but it would come. Frank and I walked out into Piccadilly Square feeling slightly dazed. This was now our home, this bewildering hotch-potch of vast grey buildings and endless streets, full of jostling, surging, anonymous people. Simultaneously we took a deep breath. What on earth had we let ourselves in for? We had no base, apart from a tiny office, no youth club, no ready clientele, no experience, no professional identity, no authority. Whatever work we did we would have to create. We had to go out there, on to the streets, and find young people in need, then persuade them that they needed us, and ultimately, that they needed Christ. The latter seemed the easiest prospect. At least Christ could perform miracles. Help, Lord, where do we start?

"The first thing we do," Frank said, with greater confidence than I thought he felt, "is to patrol the streets."

"What do we do that for?"

"To find out what goes on."

He must know. He had the university diploma in social work and I did not. So inch by inch, hour after hour, night after night, we trod the pavements, until the soles of our shoes were so worn down that I reckoned Manchester City Council deserved what we were paying in rates. We saw it all: pubs, clubs, casinos, brothels, gay bars, there was hardly a den of iniquity in Manchester which had not either ejected us or made us want to leave in a hurry. We went home feeling sad and soiled, but no nearer creating a day's work for ourselves.

One evening, it must have been late that first autumn because our breath was beginning to freeze in the night air, I stepped over a large human bundle on the pavement and walked on.

"Where do you think you're going?"

I turned round. Frank had stopped to survey the heap at his feet.

"Oh, Frank, it's only a drunk, leave him, for goodness sake." I was tired and irritated. I hated walking around in endless circles and I hated damp weather. It made my curly hair frizz.

"We can't just leave him," Frank retorted. "The next

121

bobby who comes along will book him, and that's a night in the cells.''

The stench of alcohol and vomit was beginning to waft in my direction. "Good, he has it coming to him." Frank looked at me in hurt surprise. I felt ashamed, but after all this was not what detached youth work was all about. It was romantic, glamorous, exciting, Christian Sir Galahads out rescuing the perishing!

"Would Christ have left him lying there in the gutter like that?''

Blow Frank! Blow his Christian charity!

"I'll take his arms and you take his legs. Where do you want to be, pal?''

"Hotel Piccadilly," murmured the semi-conscious form.

"Phew, we've got a posh one here," whistled Frank.

Somehow we managed to manoeuvre the heaving, retching dead weight through the streets to the doors of his hotel, then standing him on his feet, propped between us, we nonchalantly dragged him past the pages and porters, into the lift, along to his room where we dumped him on his bed and left him to snore in peace.

It was a relief to walk out into the sharp night air. I felt clean.

"Frank?''

"Yes?''

"You don't half smell.''

"Thanks.''

We giggled. "You won't find any more like that, will you?''

"I'm not promising anything.''

It was just as well he didn't. In the months that followed I lost count of the number of drugged or drunken youngsters we dragged home. But from that night on, it never bothered me. I had learnt something. The resources are within us to do whatever Christ would have done in any situation.

Not being a natural walker, and not given to enjoying the bracing winter air, I soon tired of Manchester's streets and found a little coffee-bar where I could sit in peace and while away the hours at my crochet. Occasionally one or two youths came in to shelter from the cold and I began to recognise some familiar faces. One day one of them watched me out of the corner of his eye as he shredded his paper coffee-cup. Suddenly he stopped what he was doing, caught the attention of his mates, then swaggered down over to me.

"O.K. then, show us how to do it."

"Sit down and I'll show you."

Jamo never did learn to crochet, but from that day on Frank and I rarely again had a peaceful moment. Through one lad we made contact with about two hundred young people, white, black, half-caste, unemployed, delinquent, homeless; all found a kind of refuge in the anonymity of Manchester's city streets and markets. We spent our days in the social security offices, law courts, coin arcades and V.D. clinics, but mainly hanging about on street corners, dodging police orders to "move on" just as the kids did. Some of them thought it was great. The novelty of having their own private social worker really appealed. Others were indifferent. Most were totally mystified.

"What do you really do?"

"We're here to help you in whatever way we can."

"Man, why bother? No one ever 'as before."

"Because we're Christians."

"What da you know about anyfing? Ya don't know what it's like to be black, always in da minority."

"I do know. You see, I'm a Jew and I reckon my people know even more about prejudice than yours."

"Man, you really are mixed up."

We were not exactly popular with anyone. The police were suspicious of us, the authorities found us a nuisance, the coffee-bar proprietors blamed us for the kids' vandalism and called us misguided do-gooders. There were days when I almost felt I could not face it any more. There seemed to be nothing around me but aggression, violence, injustice and gross exploitation. The world was a sickening place, divided into prey and predators. The kids were easy prey. The predators were those who plied them with booze, drugs, gambling, cheap sexual thrills and the like, all for money.

Then suddenly there were those rare moments which made everything worthwhile, like one evening at the weekly bop at Belle Vue. We were with a group of kids we had got to know well. Booze money had run out and they were bored silly. Sprawled over their chairs, the boys were discussing ways of livening up the evening.

"Ah fink ah'll go and give dat Charlie somefing 'ee won't forget. 'E makes me sick, always nicking my girls. Oo's coming den?" Darren looked slowly round, but no one looked up. Someone even yawned.

"How about turning the other cheek for a change, Darren?"

Frank's quiet words made him freeze on the spot. He grinned sheepishly. "Eh? Wot daft bugger would do that?"

"Christ would."

Darren's mouth fell open and a damp, half-chewed fag-end fell out. Gary, his mate, whose head had been resting on his folded arms, looked up at Frank slowly and blinked, as if he had seen an apparition.

"Ya don't take all that stuff serious, do yer, Frank?" he asked.

"Are them two goin' on about Jesus again?" laughed Maggie, and pulled up a chair between us.

Half a dozen more kids drew their chairs in closer, so that they could hear the conversation. Suddenly everyone was wide awake and full of questions. Who was Jesus? What did he do and why did he do it? What difference could he possibly make to the here and now? We talked on

124

and on into the small hours of the morning. The music stopped, the bar closed, the dance hall emptied, but no one moved away from our table. They were oblivious of everything except this new world which was opening before them.

"Christ said, 'If any man asks for your jacket, give him your coat as well.' "

"Did 'ee, Frank?" said Gary. "Well, give us yer jacket then."

Frank stood up obediently, took off his worn, patched old jacket and handed it over, wallet, car keys and all. My heart sank. We would never get home tonight. Gary strutted off and was gone for the next half-hour. He reappeared with a quizzical look on his face and handed the jacket back.

"Thanks, pal." Frank put it on without a flicker of emotion and sat down.

"Yer money's all there, Frank."

"Great."

"So's yer car keys—and yer car."

"Great."

Gary stared at Frank in disbelief. "You really trusted me, didn't yer? No one's ever trusted me before. Maybe you two got somefin' after all."

How did that "something" become real for those kids? For two years I struggled to find an answer. I had the distinct impression that there was a key, that though it dangled in front of our noses and was there for the taking, it belonged to the Church as the body of Christ, and not just to me as an individual. On our own Frank and I were fairly helpless. We could introduce the kids to Christ, tell them what he had done and said, and it certainly made some kind of sense to them. After all, he had mixed with the underworld of criminals and prostitutes they knew so well. The problem came when they said, "O.K. then, I'll give it a try. I'll follow Christ." As long as they fre-

125

quented the old haunts and mixed with the old company they did not stand a chance. They desperately needed an alternative, a Christian community which would love and want them. Few churches were that. If they survived one service it was a miracle. Some could not read, let alone follow a hymn book. They felt bored and awkward; they did not belong. I remembered the feeling only too well, and did not try to prevent their escape. The only comfort was that God was bigger than the failures and inadequacies of any Christian institution. We gave the kids what we could and he alone knew what they made of it all.

The intensity of the job, its utter relentlessness—a night's sleep could be disturbed at 3 or 4 a.m. by a homeless waif or two standing on the doorstep—made a long summer holiday imperative. In the Corfu sunshine a thousand bricks seemed to fall off my shoulders. I could breathe again, could exist, without glancing over my shoulder, clutching my handbag or preparing the words to deflect the next crisis. Needing some quiet I went down to the seashore in the early morning and sat on a rock, my feet dangling in the sea. Somehow I knew that my time with the Catacombs Trust would soon be at an end.

"But what then, Father? Another youth work post? I have no real ambitions or qualifications."

"What would you like to do?"

The question took me by surprise. "Well, if you really want to know . . ."

I did not have to tell him. I sensed that if I could have seen his face, there would have been a real twinkle in his eye.

9

Four years had passed since my affections were first engaged and their object was no nearer making any response now than he had been then. If anything Peter was colder, more remote. He was not unaware of my intentions and a certain stiffness had entered our relationship. He made very sure that our eyes never met across the church, that we would not end up alone together for any length of time. I found a very effective, albeit melodramtic way of coping with the situation. I imagined that in my bedroom was a little stone altar such as Abraham might have built when God asked him to sacrifice his only son Isaac. Whenever I felt I could no longer hold out Peter to God on the open palm of my hand I ran to that altar and gave him back to God again.

"He's yours, Father, and whether he's ever mine is for you to choose." Kate and Paula, my two flatmates began to respect the sanctuary of that room on many a Sunday evening.

Nonetheless, those years were anything but miserable. In fact they were very full, and often very happy. Kate, Paula and I created a real home out of our flat. Admittedly my youth work sometimes tested their patience to the very limit, such as the time we provided shelter for two homeless waifs and they left behind the two guest beds full of dead body-lice, but Paula even had the grace to comfort me. "Don't worry, darlin'," she spluttered, disappearing in a cloud of insecticide, "this stuff they gave me at the town hall should do the trick. And it not, well they're all God's little creatures, after all."

Kate was a whizz at sniffing out eligible men and inviting them back for a meal. We had quite a social life. I even received some proposals, but always my heart told me I should never love anyone as I loved Peter. It was maddening. Why could he not disappear from my life, get another job and move? Slowly the idea dawned that perhaps that was what *I* should do.

"Lord, this isn't an ultimatum," I said on my return from Corfu, when the sight of Manchester city centre was hardly endearing, "just a means of preserving the bit of sanity I have left. If there's no sign of a thaw by Christmas, I'm packing my bags and leaving Manchester," I meant it too. I had had enough.

Christmas approached, the shops glittered with goodies and the kids kept helping themselves. I was never away from the magistrates' courts. Some season of goodwill! I dreaded it. I always felt more rootless and lonely than at any other time of the year.

"Let's put up a few decorations, it'll cheer us up no end!" Kate was on hands and knees in front of the fire, sorting out a tangled heap of baubles and paper chains. The phone rang. "I'll go," she said, jumping up, "you never know, my prince may have found me at last."

When she came back into the room, I could tell from the expression of disbelief on her face that this was no ordinary telephone call.

"It's for you," she said, breaking into a huge grin. "Guess who."

My legs wobbled as I walked out into the hallway. Kate followed me. "Hello, yes? Yes, I'd love to go out for a meal. The twenty-third is free."

Paula appeared at the top of the attic stairs, drawn irresistibly by something in the air, her mouth wide open. I put down the receiver and we stared at each other in silence for a while, letting the impact of what had happened sink in. "He's asked me out for a meal." I whispered, as if the Prince of Wales himself had phoned. "He doesn't usually do that, does he?"

Simultaneously we all broke out into shrieks of laughter and cavorted round the little hallway, until the landlady's banging on the ceiling reminded us of her presence. Kate rushed to my wardrobe and rummaged around. "What are you going to wear? You'll have to buy something."

Paula was still sitting on the stairs, recovering from shock. "Well, darlin'," she said, shaking her head incredulously, "there must be hope for us all."

Within a few weeks our engagement was official. Once his mind was made up, Peter worked with the same speed and determination which had earned his beer-brewing ancestors their millions.

"I knew I must be in love," he said, "I've never spent so much on a night out in my life."

"But how did it happen? I've hardly seen you in months."

"I don't really know. Seeing you at church every week was always an embarrassment. I knew you had designs on me and I thought, 'Poor girl, she's wasting her time.' That was why I ignored you, to help you get over it. Then, a few weeks ago, I began to dislike my bachelor state. I mentioned it to God and asked if he had anyone in mind for me. I was blank at first and then I kept thinking about you, until by the end of the week I was totally distracted. It did occur to me that you might not still feel the same about me, but I was ready to take that chance."

"Not feel the same!" I hardly knew what to do with myself I was so ecstatic. I could not eat, could not sleep, was a lousy youth worker. I had only one worry. My

129

parents! How would they feel? Had I already committed the ultimate crime, or was "marrying out" still far worse?

"Poor mum," I thought, as my train shunted jerkily the last few yards over the River Tyne into Newcastle Central Station, "things never do seem to go her way where I'm concerned." There were the five bridges! I was nearly home, but this time, despite the usual apprehension, everything was different. There was someone back in Manchester thinking of me, waiting for me. I was not on my own any more.

"Still picking up yobbos out of the gutter and dropping them back, dear?"

"Yes, dad."

Supper conversation had not changed much in two years. My father, half amused, half wistful, shook his head. "If only you'd been a doctor like me. You would have made a marvellous doctor."

"What's more to the point," mum intervened, "any boys on the horizon, any nice boys?" I paused. It looked as if this was the moment.

"Yes, actually. A very special one. In fact I'm going to marry him."

"Now dear, don't get upset," my father said, patting mother on the arm, before she had time to react.

"Not Jewish, I suppose? I hardly need to ask." She was rather pale, tight-lipped, but very calm. "Well, I can't say I didn't expect it. Marry him, you don't need our permission, so don't expect a blessing either. When I think of all the dreams I've had for you."

Father waited for her to leave the table, then he turned to me. "Give her time," he whispered, "she's ready for it, she'll accept it."

I nodded, amazed at how prepared she seemed to be.

"It's strange how things work out," father continued. "Do you know, I had made up my mind to talk to you this weekend. I was going to say, 'Don't stay single just for

130

us. If there's a nice non-Jewish boy you want to marry, marry him. You'll have a life to live long after we're dead and buried. Don't sacrifice yourself for us.' However, I do have one quibble. Did you have to pick a *poor* member of the Guinness family?'' Mother came back into the room and I hugged them both.

''We can't come to any church service, you realise,'' she said, ''but we will attend a reception.''

It was more than I dreamed possible.

''Now, how shall I tell all the relatives?''

''You mean, I can bring him home to meet everyone?''

''I didn't say that. No, I'm afraid you can't. I have your brother and sister to think about. If I just give in to you they'll think they can just go and marry out if they please and it won't make a scrap of difference to us. I must set an example.''

She noticed my crestfallen expression and relented a little.

''Once he's your husband and nothing can be changed, then you can bring him home. Until then, we'll have to find a convenient meeting place somewhere half-way between Newcastle and Manchester.''

One Sunday, a few weeks later, Peter and I slipped out of church before the end of the service and drove to Harrogate to meet my parents for lunch. He chattered away easily, but I felt uneasy and tense. ''If only he knew them like I do,'' I thought. ''They'll either love him or hate him, but there's no in-between.'' Besides, the odds were hardly in his favour.

They were already there and having a drink in the bar when we arrived a little late. I hugged them stiffly, formally introduced my fiancé and to my relief they greeted him with genuine warmth. ''What a height,'' my mother gasped. To my amusement I noted that Peter was almost bent double so that she could talk to him without straining her neck. ''How tall are you?''

"Six foot four, I think. My family are all tall. Never mind," he smiled, "marriage with yours will bring us down a peg or two."

We went into lunch and there was gammon and pineapple on the menu, Peter's favourite. I wondered what he would do and watched his face with interest.

"Lamb, please," he said, then his eyes widened and his mouth fell open as father turned to the waitress and said, "And I'll have a pork chop."

"Blow it!" he whispered to me after the meal. "I could have had gammon. I was being so careful not to offend."

That was a minor surprise compared with what was to come. Over coffee my parents really got down to business. They had saved a certain amount of money to give away with their daughter, not exactly a dowry, but a little "help". Now, what had Peter to offer? How much had he saved, what did he earn and what were his prospects? I wanted to disappear into a hole. I knew that marrying off one's children still involved a financial arrangement for most Jewish parents, but I never imagined it would apply in our case. Peter looked stunned, then he rallied.

"Actually, I've saved about five hundred pounds," he said proudly.

"Nothing at all! I see," my mother sighed. "And what prospects has a schoolteacher?" She shook her head. "Well, you're not exactly all we wished for our daughter, but I suppose you'll do."

A few months later we were married in the Free Church we attended. I was disappointed that my family could not be there, especially that father did not give me away, but our church family took us to their hearts and made it a very special service. We walked out of church as man and wife on a muggy Manchester day to the tune of "H'atikvah", "the Hope", the Israeli national anthem.

To the horror of both our mothers, we bought a little wreck of a house in Didsbury, reduced it to bricks and rubble, and spent our first few years together proving to everyone that we could make it a cosy, interesting home. My parents often came to stay, especially once the first grandchild had arrived.

"You know," my mother said one evening. "I never intended to like Peter, let alone love him, but somehow he just crept up on me." Little did I guess to what extent that love was to be tested over the ensuing few months.

We had barely painted our final skirting-board, when Peter made an announcement which rocked my contented, little existence.

"Love, I think I may be called to the Church of England ministry." He was stretched out on the bed, hands under his head, staring blankly at the ceiling. I was searching for some new fascination for our one-year-old, who was never fascinated by anything for longer than two minutes.

"Great, love," I said distractedly, "a deacon in the Free Church, they'll welcome you with open arms."

"I'm serious. I've been thinking about it for ages. You know when we got married I always said I'd be in some kind of Christian ministry one day."

"Yes, but you never mentioned the Church of England. You said you didn't know what you'd do but you knew we'd never be rich. That was the day you went out and bought me the sewing machine."

There was no response. I began to feel really disturbed.

"How can we leave our church and the people we love so much? We've been members there for eight years. When I think of all that's happened in that time it hardly seems the same place."

Peter still made no reply. I allowed my mind to wander back. How rich those years had been. We were such a funny hotch-potch of a congregation, all from totally different backgrounds, Brethren, Pentecostals, Calvinists, Charismatics, Baptists. Everyone had an opinion about the church and the right to have it heard. People wrote papers on everything from "Living in a Christian Community" to "Perfect Church Government and Structures." We passed them round, studied them, debated them at General Meetings and usually decided that since there was no blueprint in the Bible we should have to agree to differ. Relationships were forged, some were severely strained, and yet a remarkable sense of commitment to one another prevailed. Changes were made, some of them quite unusual for a Free church. The Communion service became the weekly focal point for our worship, and not a monthly additional extra. Freedom was given for an extended time of extempore prayer. We learnt to be sensitive to each other, to choose appropriate hymns, to differentiate between an awkward and a reverent silence. The spontaneity and vibrancy I had longed for had become a reality. How could I leave behind what we had wept for? How would I ever cope with the Anglican liturgy, with a whole set of cultural traditions which meant nothing to me at all?

"So," I said out loud, "we just say, 'Thanks for the last eight years. We really appreciate you all very much but we've just had this sudden revelation we're meant to be Anglicans.' "

"But love," Peter said, in the supplication tone of voice I had come to recognise as saying, "I've made my mind up, so do try and accept it." It made my toenails curl. "I've explored the Free Church ministry but no door ever seems to open. I'm thirty, I can't sit around waiting any longer, not when the Church of England has issued us with such an open invitation?"

"Has it? I hadn't noticed."

"Of course. Don't you remember?"

I was blank at first and then it came to me, that weekend in Rugby! We rarely went away for weekends. Peter was the deacon in charge of the church fabric and committed to ensuring that the entire building was in perfect working order. Then close friends in Rugby invited me to speak at their

134

church one Saturday afternoon and of course we stayed for Sunday. It just happened to be the Sunday that Dr. Coggan, the Archbishop of Canterbury's appeal for men to come forward for the ministry was read out in every Anglican church, and we just happened to be sitting in one.

If ever a man's ears pricked up, Peter's did. His rigid attention made me feel slightly uneasy. After all, he was the son of an Anglican clergyman and I think I had always known where his roots really were.

"Wasn't that extraordinary?" he said as we walked back to Sunday lunch.

I feigned innocence. "What was?"

"That we should hear the Archbishop's letter."

"Ironic, yes." I had laughed and put the incident right out of my mind.

"But I'm no Anglican," I shouted, as the first awful awareness seeped like an icy pool into my consciousness that perhaps my husband was better acquainted with God's will for our lives than I was, "and I don't want to be a vicar's wife." I had visions of dowdy clothing, awful hats, of running women's meetings and organising jumble sales.

"More and more this seems to me to be the right way forward, love. We'll have to start attending the local Anglican church, of course, but we've friends there, it won't be too hard. It will give us a chance to think about it. See how you feel."

For the next few days I wandered round the house feeling miserable, unable to think of anything else. There was the Victorian pine dresser, built into the kitchen wall, which we had stripped with such loving care, and the Georgian window in the dining-room. Peter had made every joint by hand, and the little brick hearth in the front room, which we had designed ourselves, leaving the bricks to set overnight, balanced round an arched piece of curtain rail. We had rushed down in the morning to see if it had survived the night. How could I leave it all behind, to live in properties which other people had designed and decorated, never to have our own house again? It was so easy to follow Christ, wherever he asked, when there was not a lot to lose. Suddenly I realised that despite all my promises to the contrary, materialism had crept up on me without my noticing. I was enjoying a comfortable rut like so many Christians I had been quick to criticise. Giving up our home, our friends and a reasonable salary might be madness, but at least it was not boring.

"That does it, Pete, we'll go," I announced as he walked in from work a few days later. His eyes opened wide with surprise. "Quick, get in touch with the Bishop before I change my mind. After all, what is this place except bricks and mortar! God will give us another heap of stones somewhere else. There is just one thing, though, I'll try to be an Anglican, but suppose I don't really settle?"

He took me in his arms. "You will," he said, smiling down at me, "I know you will. After all, it isn't the first time you've had to make some major adjustments."

"Well, then, I suppose I'd better go and make a purple crimplene suit. Isn't that what clergymen's wives wear?"

"You dare!" he laughed.

"Oh, by the way," I called after him. He was half-way out of the door, a huge grin stretching from ear to ear. "You can tell my parents!" The grin dissolved in an instant. We stood looking at each other for a while, then he took a deep breath and nodded.

My poor parents coped a great deal better with our news than we ever anticipated.

"I knew it! I knew it! I knew you'd do something like this to me," mother raged.

"Well, after all, a clergyman is a professional man," my father reassured himself.

"Hardly one of the professions Jewish parents wish upon their children," my mother snapped.

Then gradually, despite the pain, the elasticity of their love prevailed and stretched to encompass this new shock. Mother's face slowly relaxed into a smile.

"Hmm! Mein-Sohn-in-law, the vicar! Who'd have ever thought? Well, I may yet be mother-in-law to the Archbishop of Canterbury. What would our rabbi say to that?"

A few months later, when Peter had been accepted as a prospective ordinand, and we had begun to plan our two years at theological college, my parents treated us to a few days at the seaside. The car was packed and we were ready to go, when I had an afterthought.

"Love, go and get grandma's ring out of its hiding place. I'll wear it while we're away."

"Peter," my mother commanded, "you heard the vicar's wife, she wants to wear her diamonds." When mother applied Jewish humour to a situation it was a very positive sign. "Oh, and by the way," her voice followed me out to the car, "when I die and you inherit my wonderful furs, which I've collected so carefully, I suppose you'll wear them to the parish fêtes?"

"Mother, what on earth would I want with your furs?"

"You see what I mean? That's the point. Well, don't sell them at the jumble sales, that's all, or I may come back and haunt you!"

10

I *pinch myself sometimes, just to make sure the whole thing is not some extraordinary dream.* Here I am, an Anglican, Free Church, Jewish Christian, married to a clergyman and a source of theological confusion to everyone, even myself at times. I certainly find it becoming more difficult to convince people that I am not really committed to any one particular denomination. Clergyman's wife or not I still maintain that Christ himself, not the Church of England or any other denomination, is the fulfillment of my Judaism, and if stretched to classify my particular brand of Christianity, I should probably say "Jewish." This is not mere facetiousness. Common sense and history make it quite clear that in the event of widespread anti-semitism, that is exactly how I would be labelled. Earlier this century there were large groups of Jewish Christians in Europe. After the war they were never heard of again. Conversion has never meant an easy escape from persecution. Still, I am quite pleased to be able to take a very minor stand against denominationalism, because it so undermines the credibility of the Church. It is one thing to have preferences in worship, for choice brings variety, it is another to believe that only one particular way makes a real Christian. Jewish friends say to me, "But how can you accept Christianity? Christians don't even

138

agree or get on with one another." I hang my head in shame. It is no use arguing with them that Jewish people have their feuds too. They do, but it is not the same.

When my father began to pursue in earnest his previous flirtation with Reform Judaism, the family teased him mercilessly.

"Come on, Dad," David yelped, "you know that isn't the real thing."

"Not when they have the service in English," mother laughed.

"None of my family have ever been Reform before. It sounds more like a church to me." There was more than just a hint of indignation in gran's voice. She thought she had delivered the ultimate in effrontery, but my father refused to be nonplussed. Some of our conversations had rekindled his interest in religion.

"At least I now know what I'm praying," he murmured. No one could argue the point and father was left in peace.

The differences between Reform and Orthodox Judaism, and even the wide range of opinion about practice within Orthodox Judaism, are not the same as the differences between the Christian denominations. Argument and debate have been traditional methods of learning for centuries. It is a way of life. Jews can argue furiously, even over religion, they can fight and quarrel, yet remain deeply committed to each other. This is because of a highly developed awareness of their identity as a people. The feeling of being somehow "chosen", special, and therefore vulnerable, combined with thousands of years of insecurity and suffering, have produced a sense of mutual belonging and interdependence.

I long for Christians to have a similar sense of destiny. To follow Christ is surely a special calling, the greatest privilege that ever man could possess, conferring every right to feel "chosen", but how quickly wonder evaporates, leaving behind an almost bland ordinariness about the Church. A distinguishing feature or two would help, but the one which Jesus intended to mark out his followers before the world, is the very one which rigid denominationalism throws to the wind: love. No one would wish it but I sometimes feel that until Christians have faced the harassment which has consistently pursued the Jews, they will never grasp how costly a luxury self-assertive disagreement over doctrinal accuracy really is. The threat of persecution might weaken self-reliance a little. Petty dislikes would become relatively meaningless. Christians might not take their foibles so seriously. Gentle self-mockery and humour have always been a safety valve for the Jewish people, for laughter preserves integrity and balance. Many attitudes and priorities in the church could be radically overturned. For one thing, there would have to be a loosening of dependence upon the building itself and a rediscovery of the value of worship in the home.

Jewish communities have been scattered, their synagogues destroyed, but the faith preserved as strong as ever because it did not need a building, nor even a rabbi to ensure its survival. One Jewish home is all that is required. Christians uphold family life as the key to a well-ordered society. Jews uphold family life as the key to the survival of Judaism. That is the secret of its success.

When Peter was ordained the strains and pressures of the job came as quite a shock. While at theological college we were well prepared for the fact that life would be fairly hectic, that Peter would be out many evenings and I would become a kind of clerical widow, left to my knitting and needlework. The latter was by no means unappealing. What I had not grasped was how much our life as a family would be threatened. But we were not the only ones to suffer. The Church proclaims the joys of family life and undermines it with the same breath. Families rarely worship together. The children are shunted off into Sunday

School and endless evening meetings separate spouses or mean a continual stream of babysitters.

"You're not out again, mum, are you?" Joel asked in desperation one evening. "Where to this time?"

"Church," says our two-year-old, barely able to speak.

"This can't be right," I said to Peter later. "I don't want the children to grow up thinking the Church takes their parents away from them. That's a sure way to breed resentment. When they're older I want them to associate God with the good memories, not the bad ones."

I am no more able to accept things as they are because that is how they always have been, than I could as a teenager. The only difference is that whereas it was once Judaism, now it is the Church. Must the church programme appear to treat children as an infringement of their parents' freedom, to be tolerated as a kind of necessary evil until they are old enough to sit still and keep quiet? And as for my own children, what about their Jewish heritage? Such was the pace of life that it was in danger of being eroded altogether.

One day granny brought Joel a beautifully embroidered skullcap from Israel.

He was thrilled. "Mummy," he said, examining it carefully, "am I really Jewish like granny said?"

I nodded. He put it on and looked very impressive, a real little Jewish boy. "Yes, you're Jewish, Joel, because my family is. It depends on the mother."

"But what does that mean?"

I suddenly realised how important it was that he should attend his cousin's Bar mitzvahs and take his place at the synagogue naturally and with confidence. It would be unfair to rob him of his birthright. Peter and I would have to rethink the needs of our family and find a way to hold two contrasting cultures in balance, passing on the best of both to our children.

Fortunately I married a man more convinced of the

value of my Jewish heritage than I was. For generations his family had loved the Jewish people and sought to convince Christians and Jews alike of the Jewishness of the Messiah.

"It was always Jews for breakfast, Jews for lunch and Jews for supper in my home," Peter told me that day we got engaged. "It was my father's favourite topic of conversation. Little did I guess that I was in for it for the rest of my life!"

From the first, and even more so after his decision to be ordained, Peter was determined we should hold on to my Jewishness, explore and enjoy it for ourselves and more than that, endeavour to apply some of its strengths to the Church if at all possible.

"Maintaining the Jewish culture is so important," he said to me one day with great earnestness, "that on principle I really don't believe Jews should marry out."

I laughed. "But that's what you made me do."

"I know," he said with a twinkle in his eye. "What a good job I don't always live up to my principles!"

With his encouragement I began to reassess my childhood experience to try and discover which traditions would work for us. I rejected the complex Judaic system of laws, including the dietary laws. There were far too many and they were much too complicated to observe with any measure of accuracy. And besides, I felt they were obsolete. Because of Christ's death, God's favour is a gift, not a reward. But I did realise how much I had valued the Sabbath as a family night and what it had cost my parents to refuse many interesting invitations out. Relying on their time and presence for that one evening, a special meal, familiar rituals and candlelight were part of the security and rhythm of our existence. Despite our hilarity, the festivals, with all their richness and colour celebrated around the mealtable, filled me with a sense of awe and wonder. We never closed our eyes or folded our hands in the formal way the Church often teaches children to pray, but somehow I knew God was there, in the laughter, the singing, the familiar stories and symbols, the God I was determined to discover as I grew up.

I suppose I shall never come to terms with the way Christians split the spiritual from the secular, as if there were some shame attached to being human. It still seems strange to me that there has to be a right environment, atmosphere and stance before prayer is really valid. When we were married Peter and I were told we must learn to pray together. We would spend an hour in deep discussion, then say, "We must pray about it," close our eyes and repeat the whole conversation all over again, as if closing our eyes and formal language would make God suddenly sit up and listen. I felt instinctively that prayer should be more natural, as I remembered it from childhood. Christian children learn that prayer requires absolute quiet and total concentration, then grow up banning children from church services because they make a noise.

Of course there is room for silence and solitude in meeting God. It is marvellous when the relationship gets beyond the point where words are necessary and it is enough just to sit in his presence, but a church service is not the best place. The more I see congregations huddled over their pews, each individual locked into his own private world of prayer, totally inaccessible to his neighbour, the more I understand and value the noise and chatter of the synagogue. What mattered was not the individual, but the corporate experience of worship. Physical togetherness was not a necessary misfortune to be endured. It was a vital part of communal life. My need for stillness and quiet as I struggled to feel God's presence was comparatively irrelevant. I could have my own encounter with God at home if that was what I wanted. For the Jew there is no such thing as a private religious life. His whole existence is bound up in the wider community. Every personal anniversary and special occasion from birth to death, whether joyous or sad, is celebrated in public by the entire community. No man's business is his own affair.

My grandfather's greatest pleasure in later life was to sit on a public bench on the cliffs at Roker overlooking the sea.

"Well, what sort of a day, dad?" my mother would ask him on the way home.

"Bah! No one even sat next to me," he would say with bitter disappointment some days, but on other days his whole face would flush with excitement. "You know who I met? Such an interesting man, a plumber with six children and you know how much he earns a week?"

All men were his friends. Hours wiled away at the synagogue had taught him to make people his hobby. No two Jews sit together at a service then return home without knowing the state of their neighbour's business, his medical history, favourite football team and intimate details about most of his relatives.

I would love the Church to become more of a community, knowing those moments of corporate joy and sadness which drive away loneliness and isolation. Some congregations are becoming warmer, but it is a painfully slow process, especially where there is a longer tradition of British reserve and formality. After all, where else but in church will two people who have already met sit side by side and even share a hymn book while barely saying hello? In the Church of England the only recognition that our neighbour exists at all is in the giving of the peace, a rather formalized greeting which some resent as an intrusion into their privacy anyway. The service ends and everyone dives for the door, enticed away by Sunday lunch and the church warden clanking the keys. Some Sabbath celebration!

At home we have started to celebrate *Kiddush* on Friday evenings. It is our family night, sometimes on our own, sometimes with others joining us from the wider church family. I light the Sabbath candles as my mother did, and hers before her, and sometimes I catch that unmistakable glimpse of wonder in the children's faces. We sing, eat *chollah*, drink from the *Kiddush* cup and read the familiar blessings, thanking God for weekends, but most of all that those simple symbols, bread for man's labour and wine for his rest, now remind us of Jesus. Most Jewish blessings begin reverently, "Blessed are you, O Lord, our God, King of the universe." The disciples must have been devastated when Jesus taught them they should call God, "*Abba*: Dear Daddy."

Ideally I want my children to grow up with a Jewish sense of awe for God, and the Christian joy at his nearness. I hope they will be able to express what they feel for him freely and without inhibition, not restricted by rules and formalities, either Jewish or Christian, but praying as they breathe, instinctively, because the Almighty God who made heaven and earth is also their Father.

We have the added bonus of two sets of festivals and they often dovetail. The Jewish ones are a great opportunity to recount the old familiar stories, seated around the mealtable. Christian festivals apart from Christmas seem to me to be greatly underplayed, and we try to make them special too. It is hard work, but well worth it. Easter has a whole new significance when it follows on from Passover. The *Seder* night enables all who participate to experience the last supper and appreciate how fully Christ used the symbolism to demonstrate that he was the climax of the story of man's redemption. Passover is anticipated with the same excitement as Christmas in our home and there are no presents, only an Easter egg given in exchange for the treasured *Afikomen*. The Christian symbol of resurrection replaces the Jewish symbol of sacrifice.

Peter's having no Hebrew presented a problem. In addition we received invitations to lead *Seder* nights in one or two churches. The English translation of the *Haggadah* was stilted and archaic, so we drafted our own paraphrased version, eliminating some rabbinic explanation, but closely adhering to the original text, rather than attempting to "christianise" it. Christians seem to find the evening a novel experience.

"We shall be involved in worship throughout," Peter tells the participants in his introduction, "but do feel free to joke, laugh, chat, however the mood takes you. I shall just continue."

Dozens of pairs of eyes open wide in amazement.

"What got me were the prayers," said one young man as he shook my hand vigorously on his way out. "They're just like ours."

It was my turn to be surprised. "Well, yes," I said, "many of them were psalms."

"Yes, just like ours," he repeated.

It has taken me a long time to realise that Christians have so appropriated the Jewish scriptures and worship, wrapping them round in their own cultural traditions, that they no longer recognise what originally belonged to the Jews. It is little short of pillage and plunder. Sometimes, during Communion services, I am tempted to cry out, "What have you done to our *Kiddush*?" How did that simple traditional thanksgiving, made regularly in every Jewish home, become a cold, rigid, formal occasion? Jesus never said, "From now on have a special service once a week." He simply said, "When you do this, remember me."

I often wonder how he would feel about our institutionalised Church, our Gothic buildings, quaint language and Victorian attitudes. I suspect they would be as much of a mystery to him as they were to me. As a child, although I realised Jesus was a Jew, I never really believed it, not a Jew like I was at any rate. Many Christians have totally dissociated him from his Jewishness because they believed

146

he was against it. But he was fully, truly Jewish, because he kept the spirit of the law perfectly. It was religious hypocrisy he opposed, not Judaism, and I suspect that Christian hypocrisy today would anger him as much as Jewish hypocrisy did then.

The more Christianity is put back into its Jewish context the richer it becomes. Judaism enlightens Christianity and Christianity completes Judaism. The two were never supposed to be in conflict. That is not to say that I do not appreciate the great wealth of historical tradition in which the Church of England is steeped. I imagine the Prayer Book will never call forth from me the same emotional response at the *Shema*, the *Kiddush*, or even *Yisgedal*— the prayers of mourning—yet nevertheless I am slowly learning to value the liturgy. It is good to be part of English history as well. This is still no excuse for refusing to strip away the centuries in an attempt to discover the real essence of the teachings of Jesus and his disciples, without all our cultural additions.

Many years have passed since the days when I thought I must be the only Jew who had ever become a Christian. Now there are groups of Jewish Christians all over the world, in the USA and Israel in particular, but in Britain too. I sometimes gaze at them wistfully over my shoulder. It would be so much easier to preserve Jewish-flavoured worship in a group than in isolation, but the geography never seems to work. Besides, I do enjoy my Gentile Christian family. The cross has ensured that racial differences need no longer hold us apart. And I quite enjoy being a thorn in the Church's side! The apostle Paul felt called to the Gentiles. I hope it is not presumption to identify with such a calling. So there I stand at Passover time at the supermarket checkout with the rest of the Jewish community, our trolleys filled with boxes of *matzos*, theirs to last them eight days, mine one night—at a church *Seder*! I no longer find it a schizophrenic experience. On

147

the contrary, it is twice the fun. Within me two cultures exist side by side, sometimes in tension, yet inseparable, each finding its completion in the other.

I should like to think I am a microcosm of what the Church might be. Christians continually ask me why the Jewish people do not see that Christ is the Messiah when it is so obvious! But it is not obvious to them, and never will be until they are allowed to see that Judaism and Christianity are not mutually exclusive, rather that each extends and enriches the other. For a time their Messiah is hidden from them. This is not because of some failure on their part, but a temporary arrangement, carefully planned by a God who so loved the world he had made that he wanted men of every race to have the opportunity of becoming his children by covenant. But the first agreement with his old friend Abraham will not be forgotten. God has promised the Jewish people a special part in his plans. What a day that will be. The Church had better be ready!

About the Author

Michele Guinness, the wife of an Anglican minister, was born into an Orthodox Jewish family. CHILD OF THE COVENANT, the story of her conversion to Christianity, is her first book. She and her husband live in the North of England, where she writes for local radio shows and magazines.

Bring New Meaning
and Insight Into Your Life
with

BALLANTINE/
EPIPHANY BOOKS